Robert Musil and the Tradition

of the German Novelle

Studies in Austrian Literature, Culture and Thought

Robert Musil

and the Tradition of the

German Novelle

by

Kathleen O'Connor

ARIADNE PRESS

Library of Congress Cataloging-in-Publication Data

O'Connor, Kathleen, 1949-
     Robert Musil and the tradition of the German novelle / by
Kathleen O'Connor.
          p.   cm.   --(Studies in Austrian literature, culture, and
thought)
          Includes bibliographical references and index.
          ISBN 0-929497-45-7.
          1. Musil, Robert, 1880-1942- --Criticism and interpretation.
2. Short stories, German--History and criticism.
I. Title. II. Series.
PT2625.U8Z824 1992
833.912--dc20   91-27564
                                                CIP

Cover: Art Director: George McGinnis; Designer: David Hubble

to the family

ACKNOWLEDGMENTS

Without the enjoyable dialogue with my teacher and doctoral advisor, Walter Sokel, his prompt and insightful response to my work, and his patient encouragement, this book would not have been written. I am indebted to many other teachers, colleagues, and friends for their readings, suggestions, practical guidance, and moral support in completing this endeavor: Beth Bjorklund, Tom Sauer, Gustav Pellon, Sveta Davé, John Rodden, Janette Hudson, William McDonald, Manfred Bansleben, Renate Voris, Helen Cafferty, Steven Cerf, and James Hodge. I am also grateful for the gracious welcome and willing assistance of colleagues at the Arbeitsstelle für Robert-Musil-Forschung at the University of the Saarland in Saarbrücken, especially Marie-Louise Roth and Gerti Militzer. For invaluable help with the preparation of the manuscript, I am grateful to Pete and Joanne Miller and Will Holmes. I also thank Peter Kleeman, who encouraged me from the start and is still waiting for the movie to come out. And finally, to my family, who has been my supportive base all these years, and to the newest member of it, my husband, Tom Kelly, who continues the tradition of support and love, thank you, this book's for you.

TABLE OF CONTENTS

INTRODUCTION

The German Novelle has been characterized as a closed form, a concentric structure which isolates a particular problem and then radiates a broad, though ambiguous, meaning, connoting a general truth from a particular instance. The significance of the genre appears to rest on a notion of universal or absolute truth, a metaphysical framework ordering individual cases and investing them with meaning.[1]

Robert Musil repeatedly professed a goal that would challenge this image: to assert the exception over the rule, delineate possibilities rather than define realities, transgress boundaries rather than accommodate individual phenomena to a larger order. In adopting such a goal he participated in the modernist endeavor to break out of the strictures of all-encompassing orders, to recognize and portray moments of transcendence or rupture of the closed systems by which individuals and communities had sought to explain their natural and social surroundings in the nineteenth century. Further, like many of his contemporaries in Austria at the turn of the century, Musil questioned the adequacy of language—its capacity to express the truth of a particular instance without distorting it to fit a given language system.

And yet at a formative stage of his career as a writer, Musil wrote six works of prose fiction deeply rooted within the Novelle tradition. Then, having written and published works in the genre within a period of twenty years, he devoted his literary efforts exclusively to essays and the novel, *Mann ohne Eigenschaften*, which he never completed. Musil's experimentation with the novelle and later departure from it raise questions concerning its purpose for him, the effects he sought to attain through it, and why it was superseded by other genres in his oeuvre. Examining the place of the Novelle in Musil's career serves as a means of exploring the limits and possibilities of the genre, with an eye most particularly to the question of its viability in the twentieth century.

The present study sets as its task the mutual illumination of two "careers"—that of an author and that of a genre—and as such aspires to both practical and generic criticism. It explores Musil's Novellen as a crossroads of two paths of inquiry: It examines his six major pieces of short fiction—the two stories of the *Vereinigungen* (1911), the three works collected under the title *Drei Frauen* (1924), and "Die Amsel" (1928)[2]—from the perspective of genre, seeking first to determine the significance of their roots in the Novelle tradition and to define their singular character against it. And, proceeding in the opposite direction, the study also seeks to illuminate the genre Novelle and explore its possibilities by analyzing formal and thematic structures in Musil's specific adaptations of generic conventions.

An attempt to locate works in a literary tradition raises questions of broader intellectual-historical context, and these will be pursued here as well, with emphasis on the apparent conflict between the traditional form, which might cause Musil's works to appear epigonal in the twentieth century, and Musil's modernist presuppositions and goals. In accordance with Todorov's view of genre as "the point of intersection of general poetics and literary history,"[3] this study focuses on the works of one author in a genre and interprets these specific texts in relation to literary and intellectual history and poetic theory. It thus traces several contextual threads—generic conventions and philosophical and scientific ideas—woven into the fabric of Musil's Novellen. The Novelle as genre has received little attention in Musil criticism. By far the bulk of critical work on Musil has centered on *Mann ohne Eigenschaften*, producing conclusions on Musil's views of language and literature and their theoretical implications drawn predominantly on the basis of that work. Many scholars apparently accept, implicitly, if not explicitly, the conclusion of Helmut Arntzen, "daß von [der Romansatire] her der Gesamtbau der Dichtung Musils sich erst erschließt und verstehen läßt."[4]

Marie-Louise Roth devotes one section of her comprehensive and insightful book on Musil's theoretical works (1972)[5] to Musil's genre theory. Questions raised by her subsections on each of the genres discussed in his essays—Novelle, essay, novel, and lyric poetry—serve as a starting point for the present investigation. Roth asserts Musil's emphasis on inner determinants of generic form—"eine schicksalhafte, innere Notwendigkeit" (296). She characterizes the form of the Novelle for Musil as "eine idealtypische, zeitlose Form als Ausdruck einer notwendigen, zwingenden Wahrheitvermittlung" (272).

In an article of 1973, Nanda Fischer furthers the still limited treatment of the Novelle begun by Roth.[6] Like Roth, and Musil in several instances, Fischer appeals to "inner form" as the criterion for the Novelle. Citing brevity as the only formal characteristic significant to Musil's view of the genre, Fischer holds the subjective experience of the writer to be the foundation of his concept of the Novelle. The difficulty of defining or describing "inner form" limits the conclusions of Roth and Fischer, as does insufficient reflection on the connection between inner and outer form. Moreover, neither scholar discusses the Novellen themselves. Roth and Fischer both conclude that the Novelle simply crystallizes Musil's general views on art. In some respects they are right; the concentrated form of the Novelle presents in relief the problematics of artistic representation for Musil, who took cognizance of the generic tradition. As Roth makes clear, like all writers Musil operated within sets of conventions according to and against which he crafted his own work. He chose to experiment with the Novelle at a juncture in his literary career when he made, in his own words, "die deutliche Wendung...vom Realismus zur Wahrheit" (GW7 969). Furthermore, given the marked formal differences among his works—the philosophical-psychological novel in the mode of mimetic realism, *Die Verwirrungen des Zöglings Törleß* (1906), the many essays, the two dramas (1921 and 1924), the short sketches of *Nachlaß zu Lebzeiten* (1936), the long novel fragment, *Mann ohne Eigenschaften*, and the Novellen—the question of the significance of genre to an understanding of Musil's work demands consideration.

Finally, although some excellent narratological studies of the Novellen have been completed, an examination of their generic coding can open them in a different direction. This project therefore takes up a question posed by Musil in an essay, "Warum gibt es Dichtung (u. nicht bloß Essay)?" (GW7 971), restating it and narrowing its focus to ask, "Warum gibt es die Novelle, und nicht bloß Essay?"

Addressing the role of genre in the creation and interpretation of Musil's Novellen is to embroil oneself inevitably in the issue of the significance and usefulness of concepts of genre for literary criticism in general and in the especially thorny debate about the existence and definition of the German Novelle in particular. The range of judgments pronounced over the term "Novelle" extends from firmly normative assertions (Hirsch, Klein, Pongs) to emphatic rejections of the validity of the term.[7] Even those who deny the legitimacy of "Novelle" as a category admit, however, the existence of individual "Novellen" (Pabst, Ellis) and structure their critical commentary accordingly, grouping works of this designation in their scholarship.[8] Pluralizing the word at best circumvents, but hardly solves, the dilemma. Use of the word presupposes a concept of its meaning. Its frequent use indicates, moreover, a need giving rise to it.

The need for the term "Novelle"—as for any generic designation—is associated with both critical approach and literary production. On the one hand, the term "Novelle" has served—and continues to serve—the purposes of critics, and, on the other, it illuminates dimensions of literary works overlooked or misconceived when their place within a tradition is ignored. The impossibility of arriving at an exhaustive definition of a genre or of fully explaining a text on a generic basis in no way belies the usefulness of the concept.

In considering questions of genre, critics identify and interpret conventions and expectations that bear on the production and reception of texts: Works are created and received within a tradition marked by conventions or codes. Each new work participates in conventions—inscribes codes—of one or more genres, and also deviates from these conventions, resulting in its singularity within a tradition. Readers, too, have expectations based on familiarity with conventions, and the reception of literary works is governed by adherence to and subversion of these expectations.

Alistair Fowler characterizes the synchronic dimension of a work—grammatical, literary and, I would add, generic conventions—as the *langue* from which a work arises as *parole*, a particular historical instance of discourse.[9] Attention to the synchronic axis reveals consistencies and resemblances among works, opening an avenue of approach closed off by a treatment of texts as unique artifacts. Probing the diachronic dimension of a genre reveals historical development and change, bringing to light the singular features of individual works and their implications for the tradition. A text constitutes a point on both axes and is thus a product of historical context and generic structures "sedimented" within it.[10]

Purpose—the function and intention indicated by works of a certain type, or how they ask to be read[11]—should, to my mind, occupy a central position in any genre study. Attention to formal features and their conventional use has value for the study of literature only so long as typology does not become an end in itself but is considered in light of purpose—"the unifying and controlling idea in any type of utterance, any genre...," to speak with E. D. Hirsch.[12] A discussion of genre in terms of purpose treats narrative as a discursive act, an act of communication, rather than as a fixed object with immutable properties. A focus on purpose, the ends served by a particular text, allows consideration of the relationship between story and discourse—the action recounted and the means and manner of its narration.[13]

"Purpose" is not to be equated with authorial intention, the conscious will of the author, nor with rhetorical design to achieve a specific result. As used in this study, "purpose" refers to the function of a narrative act, including its actual writing. This working definition takes into account both the agent and the audience in the interpretation of a text. The effect of a text and the response it evokes in readers are thus treated as significant aspects of its purpose in this study. And the agent of narration, most closely aligned within the text to the figure of the narrator but extending in varying degrees beyond that fictional character, sometimes in the direction of the author, will be viewed as another indicator of purpose.

The word "scriptor" coined by Barthes and discussed in his essay "The Death of the Author" is useful for marking the middle instance between the person of an author and a fictional narrator.[14] As a corrective to the strict Barthesian separation of author and text, however, this investigation into the role of genre considers the oeuvre of an author as a whole, the parts of which can illuminate each other intertextually, and whose relations to each other are of interest. Therefore, other texts of the historical author Musil will be examined not as direct indicators of intention achieving expression in a fictional work, but as intertextual illumination—one important code among many available to a "scriptor" and inscribed into a text.

The genre concept underlying this project is Wittgenstein's notion of "family resemblance," according to which objects share traits indicating affiliation among them. Each represents a variation and no complete example of the type exists. This concept can account for the roles of both object and observer in classification. It claims that works exhibit particular features, and it acknowledges the role of the observer in determining the features selected as valid indicators of affinity. The critic defines the terms of relationship—the kinds of categories she erects—according to her needs and interests. "Family resemblance" thus operates according to both induction and deduction. Because the conceptual shape of a definition is determined by the pragmatic concerns of the critic,[15] genre concepts are themselves historical.[16] A conclusion on the basis of black hair that certain individuals are related, means accepting hair color as a trait significant to a relation or distinction of interest. In another context and for other purposes, hair color may be irrelevant to classification, replaced by heart condition or IQ as a basis of affiliation when the purpose of the investigator changes.

Maurice Mandelbaum has questioned the analogy between family and genre, objecting that such traits as hair color are only external signs of the true basis of kinship, a shared genetic code.[17] Whereas his valuable insight into the difference between natural kinship and genre leads Mandelbaum to search for characteristics of objects of art that more truly correspond to genetic relations, his objection actually supports an argument for "resemblance" as an end in itself in genre criticism. No genetic relations inhere in works of literature; verbal objects have no "blood relations." "Family" remains a metaphor in literary studies. Genre classification is not an empirical but a speculative operation, a pragmatic and arbitrary, rather than natural, categorization. It is useful when considered in conjunction with purpose—the function indicated by a text and the purpose of the critic in discussing it—involving contextual and historical dimensions which play little or no part in matters of genetic kinship.

The present study focuses on some features frequently noted in practice and theory of the Novelle in hope of elucidating the purpose fulfilled by the genre Novelle within Musil's oeuvre and the place of his works in the tradition of the genre. Given the nature of the enterprise of classification and verbal, as opposed to physical, objects, an element of hermeneutic circularity—examining traits in the light of purpose and concluding purpose from the presence of certain traits and their relationships—is inevitable. The hermeneutic circuit nonetheless proves an informative and fruitful movement for interpreting Musil's Novellen and for speculating on their impact on the tradition of the genre.

We will enter the hermeneutic circle with an examination in Chapter One of the historical development of the theory of the German Novelle, in order to discern the conventions of the nineteenth century with

which Musil experimented in writing the *Vereinigungen*,
Drei Frauen and "Die Amsel."

NOTES

1. The rendering of the word "Novelle" in its German
spelling and capitalization is intended as a cipher for a
genre with a theoretical and practical tradition,
considered—not uncontroversially—over the years as
specifically German. For scholars' supporting and opposing viewpoints in the debate about the particularity of
the German Novelle, see Note 4, Chapter 1.

2. Primary texts are cited from Robert Musil, *Gesammelte Werke*, hrsg. Adolf Frisé, 2. Aufl. (Hamburg:
Rowohlt, 1981) unless otherwise noted. Citations will be
marked in the text "GW" and volume number. *Vereinigungen* and *Drei Frauen* are included in Volume 6, *Prosa und
Stücke*; "Die Amsel" appears with the rest of *Nachlaß zu
Lebzeiten* (1936) in Volume 7, *Kleine Prosa, Aphorismen,
Autobiographisches*. Theoretical works appear in Volume
8, *Essays und Reden*, and Volume 9, *Kritik*.

3. Tzvetan Todorov, "The Origin of Genres," *New
Literary History* 8.1 (1976) 164.

4. Helmut Arntzen, *Satirischer Stil: Zur Satire Robert
Musils in 'Mann ohne Eigenschaften'* (Bonn: Bouvier, 1960)
205.

5. Marie-Louise Roth, *Robert Musil, Ethik und
Ästhetik: Zum theoretischen Werk des Dichters*
(München: List, 1972).

6. Nanda Fischer, "'Eine plötzliche und umgrenzt bleibende geistige Erregung': Zum Novellenbegriff Robert Musils," *Monatshefte* 65.3 (1973) 224-240.

7. For a comprehensive review of scholarship on the Novelle, see Benno von Wiese, *Novelle*, 7th ed. (Stuttgart: Metzler, 1978). For a discussion of normative and alternative approaches to the genre, see especially 21-25.

8. John M. Ellis, *Narration in the German Novelle* (New York, London: Cambridge University Press, 1974). Cf. also von Wiese.

9. Alistair Fowler, *Kinds of Literature: An Introduction to the Theory of Genres and Modes* (Cambridge: Harvard University Press, 1982) 20. See also E.D. Hirsch, *Validity in Interpretation* (New Haven: Yale, 1967) 69.

10. Fredric Jameson, *The Political Unconscious: Narrative as a Socially Symbolic Act* (Ithaca: Cornell University Press, 1981) 140f.

11. Ross Chambers, *Story and Situation: Narrative Seduction and the Power of Fiction*, Theory and History of Literature 12 (Minneapolis: University of Minnesota Press, 1984) 27.

12. Hirsch, 99.

13. Cf. Seymour Chatman, *Story and Discourse: Narrative Structure in Fiction and Film* (Ithaca: Cornell University Press, 1978) 9 and 19.

14. Roland Barthes, "The Death of the Author," in *Image, Music, Text*, ed. and tr. Stephen Heath (New York: Hill and Wang, 1977) 142-149.

15. Adena Rosmarin, *The Power of Genre* (Minneapolis: University of Minnesota Press, 1985).

16. Ralph Cohen, "History and Genre," *New Literary History* 17.2 (1986) 203-218.

17. Maurice Mandelbaum, "Family Resemblances and Generalizations Concerning the Arts," *American Philosophical Quarterly* 2.3 (1965) 219-228.

CHAPTER ONE

The Historical Development of the Theory of the German Novelle

In his book *The German Novelle* Martin Swales accounts for formal and thematic structures in the Novelle in terms of narrative purpose, as keys to the relation between discourse and story.[1] According to Swales, "the mainspring of much Novelle writing is the contact between an ordered and reliably interpreted human universe on the one hand and an experience or set of experiences that would appear to conflict utterly with any notion of order or manageable interpretation on the other. Hence, the Novelle derives its peculiar and insistent energy from what one can best describe as a hermeneutic gamble, as a shock confrontation with marginal events" (28). In enacting and portraying a process of mediation, the Novelle responds to an interpretive dilemma. It relates a particular instance to a general order, elucidating both without reducing one to terms of the other. Thus, the Novelle has a broader aim than the short story. Concerned with the implications of an unusual happening, it contextualizes it rather than presenting it as a fragment, an isolated "slice of life." In highlighting a particular event, however, the Novelle foregoes the description,

exposition, psychological detail and reflective speculation characteristic of the novel. To a greater degree than
any other genre, it has had at its center the act of
narration, often specifying one or more casts of narrators
and listeners, relating the instance of narration to the
events recounted as a story.

Swales' account of the narrative purpose of the Novelle
as a hermeneutic venture bears remarkable similarity to
the original use of the word "novella" in Justinian law, in
which a "novella" was a case outside the existing body of
law.[2] As something new and unaccounted for, it challenged
the existing corpus and required mediation to it. It is
perhaps less than coincidence that the difficulty of
aligning an exceptional occurrence with an ordered
understanding, specifically that of jurisprudence, figures
prominently in Musil's oeuvre. In the fictional cases of the
murderers G. in "Vollendung der Liebe" and Moosbrugger in
Mann ohne Eigenschaften, as in the case of a Justinian
"novella," the appearance of truth (verisimilitude) is
raised as a question relevant to the ethical question of
justice.

The tradition of the German Novelle includes from its
inception both theoretical reflection and practical
execution. The "process of discursive and fictional
self-understanding"[3] constituting the genre arose in the
early nineteenth century. Novellas had been written in
earlier periods and within different cultural contexts, most
notably in Indian, Arabian, Persian, Classical and
Romance literature, and these forerunners did not remain
without influence on the German Novelle. Because the
Novelle assumed a unique shape and met specific needs in
the German-speaking countries in the nineteenth century,
it has been considered by many scholars,[4] whose view I
share, to be a distinctive genre of that time and place. I am
less inclined than most, however, to claim that the
Novelle lost viability as that era faded. Interestingly

enough, it is critics who posit historical limitations on the Novelle who also take pains to point out its "modernity" (Ryder, xiv; Swales, 207; Martini, 371). The "modernity" of Musil's Novellen in light of their relation to the tradition partially motivates this inquiry.

Goethe founded the German Novelle tradition in both theory and practice. In *Unterhaltungen deutscher Ausgewanderten* (1795) he employed the model of Boccaccio's *Decamerone* in both the fictive frame situation of the six narratives and in their pragmatic intent to instruct. Besides the examples of the stories themselves, the *Unterhaltungen* include explicit reflection by one of the main characters, the Baroness, on the requirements of a good story. Though she never calls the framed stories Novellen, her remarks were adopted as a normative basis for the emerging generic form.

In 1828 Goethe published a work of short fiction bearing the generic title "Novelle." His often cited conversation with Eckermann about this designation produced the first explicit definition of the Novelle: "Was ist eine Novelle anders als eine sich ereignete, unerhörte Begebenheit?"[5] Goethe's statement provides a starting point for consideration of the narrative purpose of the genre. Goethe specified that the *Begebenheit* should be actual ("sich ereignet") and yet novel, unfamiliar ("unerhört"). Because these two conditions present a conflict for the rational observer, they call for mediation.

Examination of the purpose implied by this remark proves more fruitful than the formalistic counting of "Begebenheiten" it spawned in some critical studies. Focus on the Novelle as a narrative act with a specific purpose accounts for the significance of the "Begebenheit" and for other formal characteristics which are otherwise reduced to objects of a pointless search, like the "falcon hunt" conducted in early scholarship on the genre.

From the many attempts to define the Novelle, I focus

on two features that have received repeated attention and bear most heavily on the question of narrative purpose that interests me: a distinctive tension between subjectivity and objectivity is claimed by both early theorists of the Novelle and contemporary scholars; and second, the Novelle has been perceived to have significance beyond its isolated context, to exemplify a larger "truth."

The tension between subjectivity and objectivity has been emphasized and elaborated by the Schlegels, Tieck, Ernst, Lukács, and recently by Schunicht, Swales and the genre skeptic, Ellis. The didactic character of the Novelle has its roots in the didactic genres, most particularly the *exemplum*, of the eighteenth century and entered the Novelle tradition in the two longer stories in Goethe's *Unterhaltungen*. I use the term *exemplum* in connection with the Novelle as index of the claim to connote a "truth" transcending the immediate frame of reference of a work and distinguishing novellistic purpose from primarily aesthetic, descriptive or analytic intent. Frank Ryder summarizes this claim: "The Novelle seems to say that the human condition has meaning and that the remarkable things which happen to the characters of its story are significant beyond their isolated context. At the same time, however, it gives no covering interpretation or ultimate answer. The writer does not identify his vision. The reader is wiser, but he is not in possession of the whole truth".[6] A.W. Schlegel, Tieck, Ernst, Lukács, Martini, Schunicht, and, I will argue, Musil focus on this aspect of the genre.

These two often-mentioned characteristics of the Novelle—a tension between subjectivity and objectivity and a claim to truth—bear on the issue of the transition to modernism, because they appear firmly entrenched in a nineteenth-century context, in which writers of both philosophy and fiction commonly reflected on the relation of individual subjects to their physical and social environments. The view that particular phenomena reflect universal truth belongs to an era oriented toward metaphysical systems and teleological explanations of nature and history. The late nineteenth and early twentieth centuries, on the other hand, brought the rejection of such concepts by, among others, Nietzsche, Mach, Husserl, and Freud, who questioned concepts of truth, self and individual, the substantiality of material objects, and the commensurability of language and experience. Rather than positing an overarching world order and deriving explanations of particular phenomena from it, modern thinkers sought to debunk illusion and to identify ideological, psychological, and social-historical obstacles to absolute "truth." A claim to reflect a general truth seems, therefore, to render the Novelle an anachronism in a post-Nietzschean era, in which categories of reference, validity, and extraliterary meaning have given way to emphasis on the contingency of experience and the nonreferentiality of language.

Apodictic intent seems at odds not only with modern thought but also with Musil's stated designs for literature—to transcend exhausted structures of thought and replace stagnant images of truth. The generic code of these works, however, prompts a reading of them as paradigms, examples of "truth" that challenge randomness. Failure to share this purpose would seriously undermine the bond of Musil's works to the genre. If they do share it, however, they suggest that a conception of "truth" reemerges in works of modern literature.

Tension between subjectivity and objectivity, implied by Goethe's juxtaposition of "unerhört" and "sich ereignet," was made explicit in the theoretical assertions of Friedrich and August Wilhelm Schlegel and has received repeated critical attention. Friedrich Schlegel's commentary on Boccaccio's novellas initiates this central thread of Novelle theory:

> Ich behaupte, die Novelle ist sehr geeignet, eine
> subjective Stimmung und Ansicht, und zwar die
> tiefsten und eigenthümlichsten derselben indirect
> und gleichsam sinnbildlich darzustellen.... Auf
> ähnliche Weise ist die Novelle selbst zu dieser
> indirecten und verborgenen Subjectivität vielleicht
> eben darum besonders geschickt, weil sie übrigens
> sich sehr zum Objectiven neigt, und wiewohl sie das
> Locale und das Costum gerne mit Genauigkeit
> bestimmt, es dennoch gern im Allgemeinen
> hält....(WB 41)

Subjectivity, though "indirect and concealed," was thus
declared the constitutive core of the Novelle, while
realistic detail, in any case never to override the general,
was considered secondary.

A. W. Schlegel emphasized the other structural pole,
leading the strain of Novelle theory calling for objective
realism in the genre: "...immer soll sie in der wirklichen
Welt zu Hause seyn, deswegen liebt sie auch die ganz
bestimmten Angaben von Ort, Zeit und Namen der
Personen" (WB 49). However improbable the action
portrayed in the Novelle, Schlegel held it bound to the
conditions of the real, which would restrain subjectivity:
"An die materielle Wahrscheinlichkeit, d.h. die Be-
dingungen der Wirklichkeit eines Vorfalls, muß sich der
Erzähler durchaus binden, hier erfodert sein Zweck die
größte Genauigkeit" (WB 49). His demand for realism
distinguishes the Novelle from the tradition of the short
story springing from Edgar Allan Poe's tales, in which
fantastic and realistic images clash for the purpose of
creating an aesthetic effect.

A. W. Schlegel acknowledges objectivity as a fictional
stance, however, in declaring the goal of the Novelle:

"Erfahrungen über den Weltlauf mitzutheilen, und etwas *als wirklich geschehen zu erzählen*" (WB 48, emphasis added). His formulation reveals awareness that the "objectivity," the *Chronistengebärde*, as Lukács later called it, is a pose assumed by the narrator. The appearance of objectivity is the product of a choice to narrow vision, to limit and structure the narration in a certain way.[7] By adopting a fictional stance of objectivity, the narrative subject veils his controlling perspective on the narrated events.[8] The veiling of subjectivity in an objective, realistic form leads in the Novelle to distrust of subjectivity despite, or precisely because of, the reliance on subjective control.[9] In Musil's Novellen a shift toward more overt subjectivity, and a concomitant loss of authoritative control, breaks gradually with generic conventions, as will be seen in Chapter Three.

In addition to a requirement concerning the object of representation—"das Locale und das Costum"—the other component of objectivity, left implicit in both Schlegels' definitions, is verisimilitude, a manner of narration so that the events "appear true" to a general audience. Such an objective manner depends on the universal, interpretive framework accessible to a general community of rational individuals. An unexpected, inexplicable event intrudes upon the commonly accepted order. "Truth" then, as in a legal proceeding, is that account which appears true after, and at a remove from, an original event which cannot be retrieved. The best rendering earns the status of "truth."

The intrusive occurrence narrated in the Novelle often emanates from a realm at odds with the commonly accepted natural or social order. It creates a clash and threatens rupture of the prevailing order that the narrator attempts to mediate with his subjective vision. Disruption triggers narration in the *Unterhaltungen*, in which the characters flee the chaos of revolution and create discord among themselves by arguing. Rupture, disruption, and eruption pervade the Novelle tradition, informing Goethe's "Novelle," and Kleist's "Erdbeben in Chili," "Michael Kohlhaas," and "Die Marquise von O." Forces that seem at odds with the natural order threaten the fictional worlds of Hoffmann's Novellen and of Storm's "Der Schimmelreiter," and processes of psychological eruption are portrayed in the latter Novelle, in Hauptmann's "Bahnwärter Thiel" and in Hofmannsthal's "Reitergeschichte," to name but a few examples of a novellistic clash posing a challenge to the narrator, or narrators, of German Novellen. The narrator takes on the task of mediation of the unusual, and thus proffers a view of the events from a subjective standpoint. As mediator, he structures and controls the (re)presentation of a disturbing event and thus relates it to the prevailing sense of order.

Ludwig Tieck pointed to the tension between subjective vision and object of narration by employing a metaphor of light for the Novelle. The Novelle should, he wrote, "sich dadurch aus allen andern Aufgaben hervorheben, daß sie einen großen oder kleinen Vorfall in's hellste Licht setzt, der, so leicht er sich ereignen kann, doch wunderbar, vielleicht einzig, ist" (WB 53). He implies a new way of seeing as the effect of the Novelle, a view of an occurrence filtered through the eye of a subject and conveyed in its newly highlighted form to an audience. Paul Ernst echoes Tieck's image over seventy years later in writing: "...hier wird...das alles in einem einzigen Vorfall zusammengefaßt, von dem aus das Leben dann nach rückwärts und nach vorwärts bestrahlt wird" (WB 81). The image of light being shed in various directions from a particular point underscores the subjective aspect of the Novelle, while the focus of these writers on an incident that can easily happen and would appear *alltäglich* in another context again demands "objectivity"—accessibility to common experience and understanding.

Manfred Schunicht has drawn the connection between

Tieck's concept of the Novelle and the *Totalitätsgedanke* prevalent in the metaphysics of the nineteenth century. Schunicht locates in Tieck's notion of the "wunderbar," which attains formal expression in the *Wendepunkt*, the desire for reconciliation between the subjective and the objective.[10] The "wunderbar" is, according to Tieck, the transparency of the absolute in the finite, achieved by a subject who temporarily shares the authority of an absolute, transcendent author.

Georg Lukács also held the formal control asserted by the subject to be the distinct characteristic of the Novelle, and he privileged the narrative subject as guarantor of access to the absolute. The longer epic form, on the other hand, [11] relies on revelation in and through the objective for its claim to general truth: "Die Totalität kann sich nur aus der Inhaltlichkeit des Objekts mit wahrer Evidenz ergeben: sie ist metasubjektiv, transzendent, eine Offenbarung und eine Gnade" (WB 90). In contrast, he claims of shorter epic forms:

> Das Subjekt der kleineren epischen Formen steht beherrschender und selbstherrlicher seinem Objekte gegenüber.... immer ist es seine Subjektivität, die aus der maßlosen Unendlichkeit des Weltgeschehens ein Stück herausreißt, ihm ein selbständiges Leben verleiht und das Ganze...in die Welt des Werks hineinscheinen läßt. (WB 90f)

The intense form-giving activity of the subject makes of the Novelle "die am reinsten artistische Form," and erects a "Brücke zum Absoluten" (WB 92). The basis of the Novelle in subjective control will be discussed in a later chapter of this book, particularly with regard to the modification undergone by the idea of subject in Musil's Novellen. For the time being, the access of the subject to the absolute raises the issue of the claim to "truth" often made for the Novelle and used to distinguish it from other prose forms.

The claim that the Novelle functions as exemplification, an inductive example, though indirect, even enigmatic, with implication beyond its particular context, has a long history. The concept has two central aspects—compact structure and symbolic force. Foregoing the extensive description and discursive reflection of novel and essay, it has been seen as a profound reflection of philosophical truth, differing from the purely aesthetic purpose of the short story, the unity of effect, which took its impulse from Poe's essays on poetry.[12] The German Novelle tradition, proceeding from Goethe and the Schlegels, took truth as its aim, whereas Poe held aesthetic effect, beauty, to be the highest achievement of narrative.

A. W. Schlegel introduced the concept of truth into Novelle theory. He distinguished the Novelle from the narrower didactic forms such as the fables of La Fontaine, but he claimed "a certain general validity" to be its hallmark. He argued for a genre that would serve to recount something that has no place in actual history but is nonetheless of general interest. Whereas history takes as its subject matter the progressive activity of the human race, he stated, this other genre relates that which happens over and over again, the everyday course of events, that part of it, that is, that is worthy of being recorded. To this purpose he dedicates the Novelle: "Die Gattung, welche sich dieß vornimmt, ist die Novelle, und hieraus läßt sich einsehen, daß sie, um ächt zu seyn, von der einen Seite durch seltsame Einzigkeit auffallen, von der andern Seite eine gewisse allgemeine Gültigkeit haben muß..." (WB 44f). The Novelle thus depicts not an occurrence of interest in itself alone, but one with validity and significance in other contexts.

This call for general validity in the Novelle would bar representation of history, of actions occupying a single place and time in a progressive course. Instead, it dedicates the genre to synchronic, repeated action—"was immerfort geschieht." Though bound to the conditions of reality, the subject matter of the Novelle is ahistorical. A Novelle presents a paradigm, a synchronic image that cannot be measured against historical fact or chronology.

Schlegel connects the form and content of the Novelle with the response to be elicited: "Um eine Novelle gut zu erzählen, *muß man das alltägliche,* was in die Geschichte mit eintritt, *so kurz als möglich abfertigen,* und nicht unternehmen es auf ungehörige Art aufstutzen zu wollen, *nur bey dem Außerordentlichen und Einzigen verweilen,* aber auch dieses *nicht motivirend zergliedern,* sondern *es eben positiv hinstellen und Glauben dafür fodern.*" (WB 48f; emphasis added). According to Schlegel, the Novelle should set forth its object directly rather than analyze it and should elicit a response of "faith" as opposed to rational comprehension. The aspect of response is crucial to Musil's Novellen and distinguishes them from his works in other genres. As "positiv hingestellt," the Novelle dispenses with description and analytical "dissection," tasks that belong to the novel and essay respectively.

Finally, Schlegel qualifies his definition of the didactic function of the Novelle, its goal of general validity, by stressing its indirectness: "...die Novelle, als ein poetisches Gegenbild [zur politischen Historie] ist vielmehr der Erholung gewidmet, die Unterhaltung muß in der Erscheinung oben auf seyn, und die Belehrung sich nur von selbst einstellen" (WB 49). The Novelle is not simply the illustration of a point but an aesthetic whole. Aesthetic and ethical (didactic) functions are fused; neither serves the other exclusively.

Tieck, too, ascribed a concept of absolute truth to the Novelle, valuing it, according to the Romantic ideal, as a moment of unity with a transcendent whole. "Das Wunderbare," is the moment of participation of a subject in absolute authority, which guarantees for his work an element of truth, and the *Wendepunkt* serves as the structural twist from which the marvelous truth ("das Wunderbare") emerges.[13]

Even with the historical shift in focus from Romanticism to Realism, a claim to heightened significance surfaces in discussions of the Novelle. Fritz Martini focuses on exemplification when he writes that the dominance of the Novelle of bourgeois realism rests on acceptance of the possibilty that a single instance, selected and viewed by a particular subject, can be transformed into a closed plot structure with objectifying symbolic significance. The fragmentary instance attains the force to say something about life as a whole when it is thus formed into an image.[14] Martini rightly stresses that the goal of the Novelle is not clarification or illustration of truth that could be articulated directly or systematically, but rather an allusion to something beyond the tangible and the rational, beyond the world of general understanding and experience. "Die Erzählfügung der Novelle ist nicht auf eine übersichtliche, 'allwissende' Welterklärung, sondern gerade gegensätzlich auf ein Verrätseln, damit auf die eigentliche 'Wahrheit' des Irrationalen im Leben gerichtet."[15] The process of *Verrätseln* as a means of attaining truth points to a functional analogy between the genre Novelle and the stylistic device of the *Gleichnis* in the difficult form employed by Musil, which will be discussed later.

At the turn of the century Ernst and Lukács demanded a concentrated form as touchstone for the Novelle and attributed to it a purpose beyond either mimetic representation or aesthetic effect. The abstract form of the Novelle allowed works to convey "das Notwendige" (Ernst) and build "eine Brücke zum Absoluten" (Lukács). "Unsere Novelle ist ein wahres Paradigma," wrote Ernst in "Zur Technik der Novelle" (1901/2), "...den Verfasser interessierte nur ein Schicksalsproblem, das er darstellte gewissermaßen mit der Stenographie, mit welcher etwa ein griechisches Relief ein Haus durch eine Thür andeutet" (WB 82).

In Musil's best known statement on the Novelle from his "Literarische Chronik" (1914), he affirms the traditional ascription of truth to the Novelle:

> Denn eine [Novelle] ist...etwas, das über [den Dichter] hereinbricht, eine Erschütterung; nichts, wozu man geboren ist, sondern eine Fügung des Geschicks. In diesem einen Erlebnis vertieft sich plötzlich die Welt oder seine Augen kehren sich um; an diesem einen Beispiel glaubt er zu sehen, wie alles in Wahrheit sei; das ist das Erlebnis der Novelle. Dieses Erlebnis ist selten, und wer es öfters hervorrufen will, betrügt sich. (GW9 1465)

Musil thus considers the Novelle an example, a rare experience that reveals truth. He differs from Tieck and Lukács, however, in admitting uncertainty about the nature of the "truth" attained—whether it entails a change in the viewer or reveals something inherent in the object. As evident in an early journal entry, "Es giebt keine Wahrheit, aber es gibt Wahrheiten" (TB1 12),[16] he allows the possibility of multiple truths, foregoing the claim to absolute authority included in other conceptions of the Novelle.

In refusing to dispense with a standard of truth, Musil maintained knowledge as a goal for his literary, as for his scientific and technical, endeavors. Commitment to attaining knowledge, despite lack of access to an overarching truth or to ultimate certainty, can be seen in Musil's dissertation on the theories of Ernst Mach, to be discussed in the next chapter. In his study Musil faults Mach for dismissing consideration of actual forces of necessity within nature (*Naturnotwendigkeiten*) that stimulate human perception and correspond to laws of cause and effect. Though he acknowledged scientific theories of causality as human constructs, Musil asserted confidence in the possibilty of knowing the noumenal entities giving rise to them. A view of science as the pursuit of knowledge of forces outside of human consciousness coincides with the selection of a literary genre that seeks validity in the extratextual world. The Novelle offered Musil the formal possibility of seeking and communicating knowledge through literature. The convention by which the Novelle was viewed as an *exemplum* lends his works the power of implication beyond the symbolic system in which they operate. The implicit claim to validity obtains despite the admitted indeterminacy of the knowledge attained. Lack of finality, of static "truth" is indeed part of the knowledge Musil sought to convey.

The Novelle serves the purpose of indirect, and yet "positive," means of reference for Musil. Musil's assertion (following Bela Balázs) that every artistic medium offers "eine unersetzbare Ausdrucksmöglichkeit" (GW8 1145) leads to the conclusion that the formal aspects of a genre are significant in relation to its purpose. This statement also casts doubt upon the idea that the formal characteristics of the Novelle—besides its brevity—were a matter of insignificance to Musil.[17]

Nanda Fischer identifies the "Erlebnisbedeutung," the significance of an experience with implications akin to the mystical, as Musil's measure of the value of all literature, and she claims that the Novelle simply bears the greatest potential for achieving such significance. Perhaps because her primary reference for Musil's concept of the genre is the single essay from the "Literarische Chronik," however, her argument falls short by ignoring a good deal of Musil's discussion of the genre in essays and essay fragments written while he was working on his first Novellen, the *Vereinigungen*. In addition, in claiming brevity as the single formal characteristic of the Novelle acknowledged by Musil, Fischer overlooks her own argument, proffered earlier in her article, that Musil distinguishes between the ideal Novelle and the marketplace use of the term. It is the latter common, nearly trivial conception of the Novelle addressed by Musil in citing the "Zwang, in beschränktem Raum das Nötige unterzubringen" (GW9 1466), as the only formal characteristic of the genre. In fact, Musil's ideas on the Novelle reveal far greater complexity and refinement than Fischer indicates, without approaching the rigidity of prescriptive norms.

Fischer correctly identifies limitation (the participial attributive "umgrenzt bleibend" from Musil's essay) as an important feature of Musil's Novelle concept, but she mistakenly reduces this characteristic to one of length.[18] A survey of Musil's Novellen alone might call her definition into question. They range in length from the eighteen pages of "Grigia" and "Die Portugiesin" to the thirty-eight pages of "Vollendung der Liebe." "Umgrenzt bleibend" suggests, rather, the limitation and condensation of a narrative so that it has the force of "Erlebnisbedeutung" and implies significance beyond the limited instance. Fischer is correct in stating that the Novelle represented for Musil an ideal model of literature as a whole, but it offered distinct features that make it an object of specific interest as well.

While working on the *Vereinigungen*, Musil wrote several essay fragments on genre in which he demonstrates awareness of conventions of the Novelle and compares this genre with the novel. Foremost among the features he notes are concentration, the compact form that is a product of subjective artfulness, an ideal with which he enters the discussion of the tension between subjectivity and objectivity in the Novelle. He also takes up the concept of apodictic or exemplary intent, the belief that one striking event can reveal something essential and general about human experience which has pervaded the Novelle tradition.

With his contemporaries Ernst and Lukács, Musil emphasizes extreme concentration as the "inner" form of the Novelle. In "Vorwort zu Novellen" (1911) he addresses form, specifically the conciseness often attributed to the genre: "Hier ist nur Konzentration fast mathematischer Strenge, engstes Gedankenmosaik" (GW8 1314). In contrast, the novel is marked for him by "etwas Unheiliges, Leichtgemachtes" (1313). Concentration is, Musil states, the result of penetrating beneath surface detail to the structural relations informing any phenomenon—in life as in literature.

Musil's adherence to terms of relation rather than substance indicates his affiliation with phenomenological psychology as he was exposed to it in his studies under Carl Stumpf and with emerging Gestalt theory, which will be the subject of the next chapter. His essays and journals indicate directly his concern with questions of form and genre and with the distinction between the genres novel, drama, and Novelle. In an essay fragment from 1911 Musil assigns to the novel and the drama the task of *Menschenschilderung*, of depicting temperament and character on the surface and to a moderate degree of depth. The Novelle, he continues, takes place in a profounder sphere in which the individual dissolves, is distilled out, leaving only thoughts and general relations: "Man fühlt, daß hier gar nichts mehr von einem ist, es sind dort nur Gedanken, allgemeine Relationen, die nicht die Tendenz u Fähigkeit haben ein Individuum zu bilden. In dieser Sphäre spielen die Novellen, aus dieser Sphäre, aus der Existenz dieser Sphäre holen sie ihren Konflikt" (GW8 1314). His assertion highlights the significance of structure and form to the Novelle, while assigning a more representational, content-oriented function to the longer epic genre and to the drama.

Like Lukács, Musil assigns a high value to the role of the subject in characterizing the Novelle in contradistinction to the novel. He specifies the intensity of a subjective sense of significance as the hallmark of the Novelle when he writes: "Die Technik: Zwischen Roman u Novelle steht im Dichter nichts als die Wichtigkeit.... Speziell zwischen Roman u Novelle wählt nur das Maß der Anteilnahme, das Maß dessen, was man von sich hineinlegt..." (GW8 1315). As in the theories of the Schlegels, Tieck, Ernst and Lukács, Musil views the subject as guarantor that the Novelle will attain its proper form. Not by virtue of connection to an absolute authority, but a product of its own value-giving activity, the subject remains the controlling center of the genre.

For Musil, the universal truth of the Novelle, like the truth of mathematics, inheres in general relations ("allgemeinen Relationen") and associations of meaning ("Bedeutungszusammenhängen)" rather than in a system with its validity based on a privileged origin or end. In presenting the profile of a program for art, Musil distinguishes three types of "Bedeutungszusammenhänge"—the causal-scientific, the individual-psychological (based on a single exemplary case study which can obscure the meaning behind it), and a third type, "wo man nicht das Zustandekommen sondern die Bedeutungen selbst zeigt u. wo man sie—der Kürze halber—nicht im Einzelfall zeigt, sondern im Abstrakt Allgemeinen." He consigns the second type of associational meanings and method of depicting them to the novel and the last to the Novelle (1318).

The effect of this concentrated form as its method of conveying meaning leads back to the notion of the Novelle as *exemplum*, as paradigm of something broader than itself. Whereas the novel "sagt aus und sagt alles," Musil writes, the Novelle "deutet an und schränkt ein" (Roth 468). Through limitation—the controlled selection and

distillation of narrative—and allusion—the power to
signify broadly—the Novelle achieves its effect. This
paradigmatic force is the power of myth and its purpose,
like that of myth, is to express truth. In positing the
capacity of the Novelle to portray structures beneath the
surface of empirical, psychological, and historical fact,
Musil employs the Novelle to convey truth as a set of
relations, to reveal structures of thought and emotion as a
scientist seeks to discover laws of nature.

The tendency away from mimetic representation
disturbed Musil, however, while he was writing the
Vereinigungen. The reluctance he expressed in his journal
to dispense with realism reflects the tension long noted in
Novelle criticism between the demands of objectivity,
mimetic portrayal, and a subjective vision of "truth."
Musil's struggle with these often conflicting goals will be
the subject of Chapter Three in this book.

The two strands of Novelle theory that we have
delineated and deemed pertinent to the question of purpose
in Musil's Novellen cannot be considered in isolation from
each other. Together they form the basis for the central
chapters (Three and Four) in this work. Chapter Three
explores the conflict between mimetic and mythical
impulses in *Vereinigungen* and *Drei Frauen* (with
emphasis on "Grigia" and "Die Portugiesin") as the
emergence in Musil's works of the conventional strain
between objectivity and subjectivity and as indication of an
implicit theory of language located between representation on one side and exemplification on the other. Chapter
Four investigates the role of the subject, addressing the
question of the changing concept of "subject" in Musil's
works, as in those of many twentieth-century writers.
"Tonka" and "Die Amsel" provide the textual basis for
this chapter in part because tendencies of the earlier
Novellen culminate in these later Novellen, and also
because these works address the question of narrative

purpose in the relationships among narrative subject, audience, and narrative. Musil's modification of the process of mediation enacted by the Novelle will be addressed here.

Finally, Chapter Five will shift the focus back to the question of genre and seek to locate Musil's Novellen in relation to the tradition. In the meantime, as a backdrop to a discussion of Musil's modification of the genre through his works, Chapter Two summarizes intellectual-historical currents, converging in Musil's thought, that played a role in shaping the distinctive form of his contributions to the Novelle.

NOTES

1. Martin Swales, *The German 'Novelle,'* (Princeton: Princeton University Press, 1977).

2. Von Wiese, 1.

3. Quoted is Swales' working definition of the Novelle, Swales, 18.

4. The debate over whether the Novelle is, in Theodor Mundt's words, a *"deutsches Haustier"* has raged for a good part of this century, second in ferocity perhaps only to the question, addressed in my Introduction, of whether a genre should be defined as an ideal type or a historical phenomenon. Focusing on its historical specificity, I concur especially with Swales, Paulin, and Ryder, that the Novelle was valued and developed as the product of the specific social and literary culture of Germany in the nineteenth century. The predilection for the Novelle, the high esteem it enjoyed and the development it underwent at this time and in this place distinguish it from other

European short forms, though it is related to them in some meaningful ways as well. Other scholars who have taken this position, for various reasons, are Johannes Klein, Josef Kunz, Hellmuth Himmel, Walter Silz, Fritz Martini, E. K. Bennett, H. M. Waidson, Heinrich Henel, and John Ellis.

For a cogent argument opposing this point of view, see Werner Hoffmeister's article, "Die deutsche Novelle und die amerikanische 'Tale': Ansätze zu einem gattunstypologischen Vergleich," *German Quarterly* 63.1 (1990) 32-49.

5. *Novelle*, hrsg. Josef Kunz, Wege der Forschung 55 (Darmstadt: Wissenschaftliche Buchgesellschaft, 1968) 34. Goethe's statement and others that follow that are quoted from this volume will be indicated within the text by the notation "WB" and page number.

6. Frank G. Ryder, *Die Novelle* (San Francisco: Rinehart Press, 1971) xxvii.

7. WB 362. See Fritz Martini, "Die deutsche Novelle im 'bürgerlichen Realismus': Überlegungen zur geschichtlichen Bestimmung des Formtypus," *Wirkendes Wort* (1960) 257-278.

8. Manfred Schunicht, "Der 'Falke' am 'Wendepunkt': Zu den Novellentheorien Tiecks und Heyses," *Germanisch-Romanische Monatsschrift* 1 (1960) 59. Cf. WB 443-462.

9. Swales, 38.

10. Schunicht, 48ff.

11. Georg Lukács, *Die Theorie des Romans* (Berlin: 1920) in WB 90.

12. See Edgar Allan Poe, "The Poetic Principle" and "Principles of Composition," in *Poe's Poems and Essays*, ed. Andrew Lang (1927, rpr. London: Dent, 1958).

13. Schunicht, 48.

14. WB, 370.

15. WB, 370.

16. Robert Musil, *Tagebücher*, hrsg. Adolf Frisé (Hamburg: Rowohlt, 1976).

17. These indications counter the thesis of the article by Nanda Fischer. See Fischer, 224-240.

18. Fischer, 237.

CHAPTER TWO

Musil's Intellectual-Historical Background

Musil pursued several careers and courses of study before taking up writing as his life's work. He also read extensively outside his formal education and employment, recording his responses in a journal. In secondary school and at a technical academy in Vienna, both military institutions, Musil developed interest and skills in technology. He studied engineering at the Technical Institute in Brünn and earned state certification as an engineer in 1901. In 1902-03 he served as an assistant at the Technical Institute in Stuttgart, at which time he also wrote his first (and best received) work of fiction, *Die Verwirrungen des Zöglings Törleß*. In 1903 he left Stuttgart to undertake studies at the University of Berlin that included mathematics, physics, philosophy, and psychology.[1] The focus of his studies was psychology, which at the turn of the century was in the process of being established as a field of study separate from philosophy and becoming an empirical science.

Two opposing drives vie with each other in Musil's thought: In connection with his work on the *Vereinigungen* Musil wrote, "Es sind zwei antagonistische Kräfte, die

man ins Gleichgewicht setzen muß, das dissipirende, formlose gedankliche u. das einengende, leicht leere u formale der rhetorischen Erfindung" (T1 215). Referring specifically to alternatives of style, his statement expresses one aspect of a general tension between openness and closure, dissolution and structure, potentiality and actuality, expressionistic drive toward *Aufbruch* and desire for completion that characterizes Musil's response to the strains of thought he encountered in his intellectual and cultural environment.

The intellectual currents with greatest import for Musil's adaptation of the Novelle are the moral philosophy of Friedrich Nietzsche, the empirio-criticism of Ernst Mach, the phenomenological psychology of Carl Stumpf, and its offshoot, the *Gestalt* psychology anticipated by Christian von Ehrenfels in Austria and established later by Wolfgang Köhler, Max Wertheimer, and Kurt Koffka, students of Stumpf, in Berlin. These four fields of orientation within philosophy and psychology orient Musil's Novellen in various directions; they will be pursued in the present chapter.

Musil's notebooks betray mixed, sometimes contradictory reactions to Nietzsche, whose works, primarily those published between 1881 and 1889[2] and first read by Musil at the age of eighteen, remained a decisive influence on him.[3] Nietzsche's affirmative version of nihilism—razing outmoded structures of thought to clear ground for newer, more vital, possibilities—laid the foundation for what has been termed negativity and utopianism in Musil's works. Rather than erecting a structure to define, reflect, or embody truth, Nietzsche proclaimed the need to strip away illusions and expose the false premises of prevailing sytems of "truth," particularly moral systems imposing constraints on action. He rejected the conventional understanding of truth as fidelity to a world of extra-linguistic "facts."

The character "monsieur le vivisecteur" in Musil's first journal can be seen as an apprentice in the Nietzschean profession of philosophy as vivisection. In *Jenseits von Gut und Böse* Nietzsche praises the philosophers who serve as the "bad conscience of their time": "Indem sie gerade den Tugenden der Zeit das Messer vivisektorisch auf die Brust setzten, verriethen sie, was ihr eignes Geheimniss war: um eine neue Grösse des Menschen zu wissen, um einen neuen ungegangenen Weg zu seiner Vergrösserung. Jedes Mal deckten sie auf, wie viel Heuchelei, Bequemlichkeit, Sich-gehen-lassen und Sich-fallen-lassen, wie viel Lüge unter dem bestgeehrten Typus ihrer zeitgenössischen Moralität versteckt, wie viel Tugend überlebt sei."[4] Nietzsche's view that the truth of a proposition depends on the perspective from which it is uttered, and his insistence on variable, dynamic, and multiple concepts of truth, inform Musil's view, summarized most succinctly in his remark, "Es giebt keine Wahrheit, aber es giebt Wahrheiten" (T1 12). His fiction reflects the denial of a single absolute truth.

That early comment already contains the seeds of difference from Nietzsche's position, however, namely in the acceptance, even in the plural, of "truths." Musil indicates frustration with Nietzsche's inability or unwillingness to progress beyond the delineation of possibilities to a further stage where some degree of completion, realization, and even testing of possibilities could be achieved. Out of dissatisfaction with the limits of Nietzsche's accomplishment, indicated in the following journal entries and later qualified as "Jugendliche Anmaßung" (T1 50), Musil attempted to fulfill expectations raised by Nietzsche. In both passages Musil first lauds the visions proclaimed by his mentor and then laments the failure to realize them: "Das Charakteristische liegt darin, daß er sagt: dies könnte so sein und jenes so. Und darauf könnte man dies und daran jenes bauen. Kurz er spricht von lauter Möglichkeiten, lauter Combinationen, ohne eine einzige uns wirklich ausgeführt zu zeigen" (T1 12). A passage bearing the heading "Etwas über Nietzsche" reveals his strongest note of disappointment:

> Man nennt ihn unphilosophisch. Seine Werke lesen sich wie geistreiche Spielereien. Mir kommt er vor wie jemand der hundert neue Möglichkeiten erschlossen hat und keine ausgeführt. Daher lieben ihn die Leute denen neue Möglichkeiten Bedürfnis sind, und nennen ihn jene unphilosophisch die das mathematisch berechnete Resultat nicht missen können. Nietzsche an sich /Jugendliche Anmaßung/ hat keinen zu großen Wert. Nietzsche aber und zehn tüchtige geistige Arbeiter, die das thun, was er nur zeigte brächten uns einen Culturfortschritt von tausend Jahren. (T1 50)

If Musil ventured to become one of the "zehn tüchtige geistige Arbeiter" who would carry out Nietzsche's failed program, it was Nietzsche who also suggested the means of doing so. In proclaiming fiction, artifice, and mythmaking as activities superceding the pursuit of preexistent truth, Nietzsche championed creativity as a means to knowledge that must supplement (and would, in Musil's view, itself need supplementation by) an empirical approach. Nietzsche thus assigned to art a status equal to that of science in the pursuit of knowledge. The Nietzschean fusion of science and art underlies Musil's approach to his own writing, as when he sees the "Gedanken zur 'Wissenschaft vom Menschen'" collected in his diary as implying "die große Frage des Stils" (T1 137). Musil held the task of the artist to be delineation of form, a process comprising both creativity and recognition of form inherent in an object or situation. His exploration of the possibilities of generic form thus entailed an inquiry into art as a means to knowledge of the world and into his own identity and purpose as an artist.

The perspectivism of Nietzsche's epistemology shapes Musil's moral philosophy as well, in which the priority of fact and value is reversed and both are relativized. If, as Nietzsche claimed, every fact is already an interpretation, then all knowledge has an ethical dimension. Nietzsche sharply distinguished ethics from morals, a system of values forcing ethics into dogmatic categories serving particular interests. Attacking belief in absolute moral values, he replaced categories such as good and evil with the single category of power (*Macht*). Power and productivity served as his measures of value. Assuming the perspective of the whole, of life itself, rather than that of the individual, Nietzsche recast the notions of good and evil into an opposition between life-enhancing and life-thwarting forces.[5]

In a notebook entry Musil echoes Nietzsche's condemnation of conventional moral values and his affirmation of energy-producing expansion, regardless of direction: "Wir Andern, wir Immoralisten haben umgekehrt unser Herz weit gemacht für alle Art Verstehn, Begreifen, Gutheißen. Wir verneinen nicht leicht, wir suchen unsere Ehre darin, Bejahende zu sein" (T1 33). Musil described the *Vereinigungen* as his attempt to pursue "den Weg der kleinsten Schritte," which, he wrote, "hat einen moralischen Wert: die Demonstration des moralischen Spektrums mit den stetigen Übergängen von etwas zu seinem Gegenteil" (GW 7 972). The Nietzschean imperative to revaluate moral values was further carried out by fictional characters who were brought, in Musil's words, "zur Erkenntnis des Wertes der Lüge, der Einsamkeit, der Untreue in der Liebe" (T1 214).

In weighing value and power, Musil assumed a more individualistic perspective than Nietzsche's holistic vitalism, while he also held a more flexible, open view of the "individual" than that of contemporary humanistic science and philosophy. Musil's ambivalence toward the "self" as unified, centered subject and his adaptation of Nietzsche's and Mach's skepticism toward it, will be discussed later in this chapter and explored in detail in Chapter Four. His persistent effort to render experience from an inner perspective, however, and frequent reference to "soul" suggest that Musil viewed the locus from which value is determined as a "center" of sorts, not as substance but as a field of intellectual and emotional energy cohering, however provisionally, around an individual. He prized whatever is of value to the soul ("seelisch von Wert" [GW7 972]), that which intensifies or expands the soul—the nonrational dimension of the psyche and counterpart to rational intelligence. An ethical awakening, he writes, entails at once loss and gain of self: "Das Wollen löst sich, wir sind nicht wir selbst und doch zum erstenmal wir selbst"(GW8 1017). The ethical condition consists in wakening and ascending and is determined by whether the development of the soul ("das Werden der Seele") is inhibited or enhanced.

Nietzsche's psychology of drives became a significant thread, interwoven with many others, in the psychological texture of Musil's work. Like his views on truth and ethics, Nietzsche's psychology centered on the concept of power. Psychological strength, Nietzsche claimed, grows out of tension between opposing drives; opposition between drives leads to decadence, which, if overcome, produces the greatest strength. This productive dialectical tension informs "Vollendung der Liebe," where intense feeling for a distant lover (*Fernliebe*) stands in erotic tension with repulsion toward one near at hand, and "Die Portugiesin," in which severe illness serves as a necessary condition for extraordinary physical strength.

For Musil psychic processes have a dimension beyond the conventionally psychological. He distinguishes his own goals and methods from those of systematic, rational psychology, and from psychoanalysis, despite the similar concern of the latter with drives as determinants of psychic activity. Like Nietzsche, Musil refused to separate psychology from ethics. His position became clear as he wrestled with the *Vereinigungen* and declared a turn "Von der Psychologie, die ein realistisches Element ist, zu etwas ihr Ähnlichem und doch von ihr gründlich Verschiedenem" (GW7 969f). In these Novellen, he claimed to seek "die wahren (ethischen, nicht bloß psychologischen) Determinanten des Handelns" (T1 232), assigning ethical considerations a place in psychology in the broad sense of Nietzsche's *Menschenkenntnis*.[6]

A second aspect of Nietzschean psychology resonates in a major strain of Musil's work—the interpenetration of feeling and thought, rational and aesthetic faculties. Musil sought to preserve the energy of affective response without sacrificing intellectual rigor. On one front he derided "die große Schlamperei des Denkens" (T1 21), the price of overemphasis on the sensual, which he condemned as unfruitful, and on another he warned against an "Überschätzung der Vernunft" (T1 32). Musil embraced a dialectical notion of knowledge in which thought and feeling are both engaged: "Es erinnert an Platos: Erkennen—Wiederkennen. Auch speziell...an folgenden Gedankengang: Alles, was von der 'Seele' ausgesagt wird, versteht man nicht mit dem Verstande, so wie man wissenschaftliche Philosophie mit der nötigen Aufmerksamkeit immer versteht. Die bezüglichen Gedanken sind halbe Gefühle; man versteht sie, wenn das betreffende Gefühl in einem selbst wach wird" (T1 148). Both poles of what Musil called, borrowing from Novalis, the *senti-mental* (GW8 1008, 1336), the mutual reinforcement of reason and emotion in attaining knowledge, inform characters, plot conflicts, and narrative technique throughout Musil's works.

In the same decade in which Nietzsche's middle and late work appeared, Ernst Mach published *Analyse der Empfindungen* (1886). Musil attended lectures by Mach, read many of his works, and submitted a critique of his thought as a dissertation under Stumpf in Berlin. Mach drew epistemological conclusions from the standpoint of empirical science that correspond in large measure to Nietzsche's philosophical critique of the concepts "subject" and "object." Trained in the empirical method, Mach, like many scientists, philosophers, and writers at the end of the nineteenth century, focused on the subjective "screen," the "temperament" proclaimed by Zola as mediator of reality.

In *Analyse der Empfindungen* Mach asserted that the only objects of knowledge accessible to consciousness are sensations. The existence of substances presumed to produce them cannot be verified, tested, or measured in any way. The self, objects, and forces such as causality cannot, therefore, give rise to valid knowledge. These entities are, rather, categories imposed onto sensations by the mind. The structures by which the mind organizes sensations, "elements" as Mach called them, are purely heuristic, economic terms serving pragmatic ends. Elements are neither subjective nor objective since Mach's sensationalism erases the duality between mind and matter, inner and outer "reality," self and world. The goal of science, according to Mach, is analysis, breaking down phenomena in order to identify their constitutive elements. Synthesis into larger entities and attribution of substance to these groupings were regarded as acts of faith, untenable for the modern thinker.

Musil shared many of Mach's premises but differed from him in some respects as well. Awareness of both advantages and disadvantages of analysis of experience into basic elements informs his sketch "Triedere" published in *Nachlaß zu Lebzeiten* (1936). The narrator of this reflection observes an office building across the street through a telescope. Focusing on the business hours posted at the door calls attention to the absence of human activity, which, despite its usualness, suddenly seems strange. The windows and pillars of the building itself appear different: "[er] erschrak beinahe vor der steinernen perspektivischen Korrektheit, mit der sie zu ihm herüberblickten" (GW7 519). Everything in his field of vision—a streetcar, women, items of clothing, a man's hat—changes when the narrator isolates it from its context by means of the optical device: "Man sieht die Dinge immer mitsamt ihrer Umgebung an und hält sie gewohnheitsmäßig für das, was sie darin bedeuten. Treten sie aber einmal heraus, so sind sie unverständlich und schrecklich, wie es der erste Tag nach der Weltschöpfung gewesen sein mag, ehe sich die Erscheinungen aneinander und an uns gewöhnt hatten" (GW7 520f). The speaker/voyeur pronounces an ambivalent judgment on his "weltanschauliches Werkzeug," however, in stating, "Auf solche Weise trägt also das Fernglas sowohl zum Verständnis des einzelnen Menschen bei als auch zu einer sich vertiefenden Verständnislosigkeit für das Menschsein" (522).

In his speech on the poet Rilke, Musil points to the benefit of looking at the whole, the larger context. He praises Rilke's poetry for revealing the connections, the "sonderbare Beziehungen" among phenomena that connect them like the figures within the whole pattern of a carpet. And his ironic depiction at the opening of *Mann ohne Eigenschaften* of a "beautiful August day in the summer of 1913" in technically precise meteorological detail raises the question whether the exact knowledge gained by close inspection of minutiae outweighs the loss of a view of the whole and of the relations among elements within a context.

Vacillation between a positive and negative valuation of analysis into dissolute elements becomes evident in

Musil's images of the "self" in the Novellen as well. These works explore the freedom implied by a view of the self as a free-flowing stream of perceptions and thoughts rather than as a stable entity, yet they also constitute an effort toward a "salvage of the self," to speak with Peter Berger.[7] Musil counters the delight of many of his contemporaries in the concept of "das unrettbare Ich" by according equal attention and assigning reality to groupings and forms assumed by sensations, even when they are labile, unstable, and provisional.[8]

Out of concern for the potential dissolution entailed by analyzing phenomena into elements and examining these in isolation from the whole, Musil opposed literary and cultural decadence, which he associated with Schopenhauer and Wagner. Dissecting experience into isolated elements could lead, he feared, to "decad: das verarmte Leben, der Wille zum Ende, die große Müdigkeit" (T1 27). Quoting from Nietzsche's *Der Fall Wagner*, he wrote in his journal:

> Womit kennzeichnet sich jede literarische decadence /Vereinigungen/? Damit, daß das Leben nicht mehr im Ganzen wohnt. Das Wort wird souverain und springt aus dem Satz hinaus, der Satz greift über und verdunkelt den Sinn der Seite, die Seite gewinnt Leben auf Unkosten des Ganzen, —das Ganze ist kein Ganzes mehr. Aber das ist das Gleichnis für jeden Stil der decadence: jedes Mal Anarchie der Atome, Disgregation des Willens, 'Freiheit des Individuums,' moralisch geredet.... Das Leben, die gleiche Lebendigkeit, die Vibration und Exuberanz des Lebens in die kleinsten Gebilde zurückgedrängt, der Rest arm an Leben....Das Ganze lebt überhaupt nicht mehr: es ist zusammengesetzt, gerechnet, künstlich, ein Artefakt. (T1 28f)

As a hedge against the "anarchy of atoms," Musil posed structure, deriding, in Nietzschean terms, "[d]as Gemeinsame in Wagner und 'den andern'...: Der Niedergang der organisirenden Kraft;...die Überlebendigkeit im Kleinsten" (T1 29). In this passage in his journal he goes on to criticize emotional affect at any price, refinement as an expression of impoverished life, and the increasingly prevalent emphasis on nerves rather than flesh (T1 29). While he accepted Nietzsche's identification of insufficient trust in the instincts as a symptom of decadence (T1 32), Musil added a caveat to an otherwise approving citation of Nietzsche: "Trotzdem wird man oft die Instinkte corrigiren müssen..." (T1 32).

The phenomenological psychology of his teacher Carl Stumpf supplied Musil with fuel for a corrective drive against decadence. Three notions in particular with which Musil countered trends toward dissolution can be traced to Stumpf. The first of these, act psychology, originated with Stumpf's mentor, Franz Brentano, and was defined in opposition to the "psychology of content" of Wilhelm Wundt. Second, Musil employs Stumpf's epistemological premises in answer to Mach's sensationalism, taking a stance between the two by claiming correspondence between logical and natural laws. The third concept, that of *Gestalt* theory, in which form is considered an integral quality, distinct from and greater than the parts of a whole, may have informed Musil's reception of the Novelle tradition and his experimentation with the genre.

Phenomenological psychology is an empirical science with experience as its object.[9] It proceeds inductively, acknowledging sensual evidence rather than dogmatic or theoretical schemas as a basis for explanation of psychic processes. The phenomenological psychologist accepts introspection and direct report of personal experience as legitimate evidence of psychic activity and particularly as a means of access to experience not adequately reflected in behavioral or physiological response. Wilhelm Wundt, one of its forerunners and a major pioneer of modern psychology, had investigated the sensory content of immediate experience by a method of introspection and analysis. The units into which he analyzed experience were called "true sensations" or "contents of consciousness."[10] Valuing experiential data only when observed and quantified under controlled conditions, he introduced the experimental method into psychology.

Against the atomism of Wundt's psychology of content, Brentano, who taught in Vienna from 1874 to 1894, posited a psychology of act, proclaiming intentionality, rather than elements of sensation, as the essence of experience. According to Brentano, psychic phenomena, which he called acts, possess "immanent objectivity," that is, their objects exist within them. For example, color exists within the act of seeing, and "seeing" has no meaning without an object (as opposed to physical phenomena which are self-contained and have neither objects nor intentions.)[11] In identifying two components of psychic phenomena, intention and object, Brentano maintained a dualism between physical and mental facts, between matter and mind. His intellectual legacy was a psychology of experience that distinguished itself from the physical sciences, whereas Mach and Wundt held the distinction between psychology and physics to be nothing more than a difference in perspective. Brentano classified psychic acts into the categories ideating (sensing, imagining), judging (for example, perceiving, recalling, rejecting), loving or hating.[12]

Stumpf incorporated experiment into the phenomenological approach in his important research into the psychology of sound, but like his friend and teacher Brentano, he differed with Wundt on its value, arguing that theoretical knowledge of music is as necessary as laboratory experimentation to understanding the perception of tone. Stumpf's refusal to rely solely on experimentally verifiable data reflected Brentano's view that too great a stress on experimentation led to "an overemphasis upon method, and a failure to see the psychological wood for the methodological trees."[13] Stumpf followed Brentano in focusing on experience as an *act* of the mind rather than as its *content*. He treated experience as a process and sought to describe that process as a whole.

Stumpf accepted a dualism of mind and nature but held that the mind perceives substance and causal relations as they exist in nature rather than adding them to sensation in a separate mental act. He maintained that truth manifests itself to consciousness as self-evidence, thereby admitting a subjective aspect to knowledge, but he considered truth a function of the object, not the subject, the thought, not the thinker.[14]

In his dissertation, *Beiträge zu einer Beurteilung der Lehren Machs* (1908),[15] Musil delineates a position between Mach's skepticism and Stumpf's optimism concerning the possibility of direct knowledge of objects and their relations. Musil accepts Mach's claim that science, including psychology, only describes facts and the functional relations between them, predicting when one event will follow another. He explicates Mach's view that there is no direct access to a given truth, no self-evidence, and hence no determinate knowledge or truth independent of mental categories. He asserts his own view, however, that the laws of logic according to which the mind formulates natural laws, are, in fact, psycho-logical laws compelled by forces just as real as (though no more so than) other natural forces.

Musil applies Stumpf's epistemological premises as correctives to Mach's, by arguing that logical constructs correspond to the regularities in nature that give rise to them: "Die Erfahrung nun lehrt das Bestehen ungeheurer Regelmäßigkeiten mit Deutlichkeit erkennen. Diese Regelmäßigkeit, die uns zuallererst auf eine Notwendigkeit schließen läßt, liegt also in den Tatsachen" (BBLM 122f). Despite the lack of direct connection between logic and natural forces, logical conclusions, of substance or causality for example, are nonetheless derived from observation of natural phenomena and thus justified by a factual basis: "[Die Notwendigkeit] setzt freilich vorerst eine Idealisierung voraus, die ist aber auch nicht die eigentliche Notwendigkeit, ja sie ist überhaupt nur Notwendigkeit, wenn es zuerst jene andere gibt, die in den Tatsachen liegt, selbst wenn wir mit unseren Mitteln an deren wahre Struktur nie ganz herankommen sollten" (BBLM 123). Musil's claim that knowledge has a basis in external reality implies acknowledgment of an aspect of truth independent of the mind. Although science cannot attain final certainty, its propositions are, according to his dissertation, more than economic (*denkökonomische*) fictions; their truth value can be judged. Musil counters the epistemological skepticism of Mach's positivism with a firm realism—the confidence that experience can impart knowledge.

Musil's critique of Mach thus represents one aspect of an attempt to identify forces that constrain and structure the creative activity of the psyche and so bring the possibilities proclaimed by Nietzsche to a stage of completion. The connection he posited between psychic and physical phenomena and his refusal to conflate them into a monistic principle countered the danger he perceived in the view, symptomatic of decadence, that experience consists of a chaos of disordered sensations. Act psychology provided another hedge against dissipation by viewing experience as a process of intentionality, of interaction between subject and object that cannot be reduced.

The third concept providing an intellectual basis for the synthetic impulse Musil applied in resistance to the excessive concentration on analysis is *Gestalt* psychology. The idea of *Gestalt* had a direct bearing on Musil's concept of form and can be seen to have influenced his understanding of the Novelle and to have motivated his choice of that tighter generic form before he devoted himself to the more inchoate, and ultimately unfinished, novel.

Christian von Ehrenfels, a student of Brentano in Vienna, had introduced the concept of *Gestaltqualität* into the discussion of positivism. In a treatise published in 1890,[16] he had contended that form does not inhere in the elements of a phenomenon themselves but in their association. His emphasis on form as an essential component of sensation and his insistence on form as function rather than content reveal the roots of his concept of experience in the act psychology of his teacher, Brentano.

Gestalt theory received further decisive impulse from Stumpf's concept of act psychology. Stumpf had continued Brentano's discussion of psychic acts, renaming them "functions." Addressing the question of Brentano's "immanent objectivity," Stumpf posited *Gebilde*, "formations," possessing both qualitative and relational dimensions, as the objects of functions.[17] Functions thus included their objects and could not be analyzed into smaller components.

Stumpf's pupils, who defined and developed *Gestalt* theory, adopted his view of consciousness as consisting in nonreducible acts. Refusing to acknowledge elements, the end-products of the analysis of perception, as real, Köhler, Wertheimer, and Koffka founded the psychology of *Gestalt* in 1912 in Berlin. Musil became familiar with ideas of *Gestalt* in its early forms in Berlin and maintained an interest in it especially through contact with fellow student and lifelong friend, Johannes von Allesch, whose academic pursuits included applying *Gestalt* theory to Stumpf's tone psychology and the visual arts.[18]

In his book *Gestalt Psychology* (1929), Wolfgang Köhler pursues several ideas that have significant parallels in Musil's work. He takes issue with Wundt's goal of analyzing experience into "true sensations," arguing that psychology should explore the qualitative dimension of behavior neglected in exclusively quantitative methods. Reliance on quantifiable samples of behavior, he claims, restricts knowledge of the psyche by excluding many behavioral possibilities from scientific investigation, gaining exactness at the price of sterility.[19] Wundt's reductive method neglects the character of common experience, in which the whole is truer than artificially isolated elements.[20]

Musil defined and discussed the concept of *Gestalt* in an essay written in 1931 entitled "Bedeutung der Form." The significance he attached to it can be seen in the following passage:

> Er bedeutet, daß aus dem Neben- und Nacheinander sinnlich gegebener Elemente etwas entstehen kann, das sich nicht durch sie ausdrücken und ausmessen läßt....So besteht, als eines der einfachsten Beispiele, ein Rechteck zwar aus seinen vier Seiten und eine Melodie aus ihren Tönen, aber in deren einmaligem Stand zueinander, der eben die Gestalt ausmacht und einen Ausdruck hat, der sich aus den Ausdrucksmöglichkeiten der Bestandteile nicht erklären läßt. Gestalten sind...nicht ganz irrational, denn sie lassen ja Vergleiche und Klassifizierungen zu, aber sie enthalten doch auch etwas sehr Individuelles, ein So und nicht wieder. (GW8 1218)

Musil points to the pragmatic advantage of experiencing phenomena as synthetic wholes. People learn to bundle isolated perceptions and impulses into wholes, he writes, as in basic *Gestalt* formation, in order to master life's tasks (1219). They create formulas as an economic means of simplifying problems, conserving effort, and minimizing discomfort. For example, he adds with a humorous touch, one glosses over the many disturbing details of a complicated dental operation with the unrevealing (and, thankfully, narcotic) term, "root canal" (1220). A person who cannot execute such economic maneuvers becomes neurotic, he insists.

There are, however, in Musil's view, drawbacks to this readily synthetic mode of perception. The economic operations of the mind can flatten experience, particularly when one constellation governs subsequent experiences by force of habit and thus obscures or distorts unfamiliar perceptions and novel constellations. People understandably resist the dissection of the formulas of feeling and thought that help them cope with the world, Musil writes, but, on the other hand, excessive acceptance of preformulated "whole" facts is just as characteristic of stupidity, especially moral stupidity, as is the excessive splintering of perception indicative of debility of character (1221f). His reservation recalls an earlier journal entry in which he had warned against "Denk-Gewohnheiten," habits of thought, which he had called the most invisible and rigid barriers (T1 23).

The idea of *Gestalt* as expounded by both Musil and Köhler provides an antidote to the invidious limitations of *Denk-Gewohnheiten* and the sterility of formulaic perception. The dynamic quality that both men attribute to *Gestalt* formation preserves the quality of flux, variability, and movement in Mach's sensualism, while recognizing shapes and rhythms, the forms in which sensations appear. In Köhler's words, "This indeed is the most general concept of *Gestalt* psychology: wherever a process dynamically distributes and regulates itself, determined by the actual situation in a whole field, this process is said to follow principles of Gestalt theory."[21] Thus, *Gestalt* allows a compromise between fluidity and form, stagnation and formlessness, that informs Musil's approach to language and its capacity to convey meaning. It likewise affects his choice of genre and style.

In the essay "Bedeutung der Form" Musil draws a further connection between the concept of *Gestalt* and that of self. A new psychology of the self, he writes, is gradually taking the place of the traditional, rationalistic schema of the soul that has been formed arbitrarily in the image of logical thought (1221), the "individual" at the center of the bourgeois worldview. The newly conceived self is decentralized; it acts not as a stable consciousness making rational, pragmatic decisions, but rather as a field of complex reactions which it justifies only in retrospect by acts of consciousness. (Any similarity to Freud's precepts is denied at this juncture with a footnote warning against confusing this idea with principles of psychoanalysis.) Musil applauds the view of the self as a dynamic process, a (changeable) shape assumed by reactions in flux, not as a loss but as a strengthening of the self:

> Das ist nicht im Sinn einer "Enthauptung" zu verstehn, im Gegenteil, die Bedeutung des Bewußtseins, der Vernunft, der Person usw. wird dadurch gekräftigt; trotzdem verhält es sich so, daß der Mensch bei sehr vielen und gerade den persönlichsten Handlungen nicht von seinem Ich geführt wird, sondern dieses mit sich führt, das auf der Lebensreise durchaus eine Mittelstellung zwischen Kapitän und Passagier innehat. (1222)

The image of the self as occupant of a middle ground between captain and passenger on life's journey marks Musil's quest for a concept of self that balances activity and passivity, substance and flux, one that does not limit freedom and yet refuses to dispense with the self as "unrettbar."

Musil concludes the essay on the concept of *Gestalt* with a comparison to language. His comment raises the final topic of the present discussion of the intellectual-historical currents in his Novellen. He writes, "daß das einzelne, der Satz und Satzteil, seine Bedeutung nicht an und für sich, sondern erst durch seine Stellung im Ganzen hat" (1224). Though written in 1931, his statement remains consistent with the entry in an early notebook, in which, citing Nietzsche, he characterizes literary decadence as a loss of the whole and locates meaning in the relations among word, sentence, and work, using syntax as a model for the significance of the whole over that of individual elements.

The principle of *Gestalt* informs Musil's response to the skepticism toward language prevalent at the turn of the century. Philosophical and fictional texts by writers of the late nineteenth and early twentieth centuries including Kierkegaard, Nietzsche, Mauthner, Maeterlinck, Hofmannsthal, Kraus, Wittgenstein, Kafka, and Broch questioned the correspondence of language to inner and outer reality while often declaring, on the other hand, the urgency of such expression.

In his now famous essay entitled "Über Wahrheit und Lüge im extra-moralischen Sinn," Nietzsche had asserted the inevitable metaphoricity of all language, the lack of a natural connection between word and referent. Nietzsche celebrated the creative possibilities and freedom entailed by the artifice of language and condemned the petrifaction of metaphors into immutable concepts. By contrast, Mauthner lamented the gap between reality and thought that precluded the possibility of philosophical and scientific truth and limited man to knowledge of appearances only, rather than of real entities. Hofmannsthal's fictional Lord Chandos decries the dissolution of the unity he had formerly perceived in nature, within which language existed and enabled contact between the mind and the material world, and the loss of correspondence between language and experience, word and object. Karl Kraus, by contrast, professed faith in the congruence between language and life, but he crusaded against the abuse of the German language, particularly in journalism.

In the *Tractatus Logico-Philosophicus* (1921), Wittgenstein assigned limits to language, consigning philosophers to silence in the spheres of ethics and metaphysics. These, he maintained, transcend the speakable. Hofmannsthal, Broch, and Musil sought alternative means of expressing the inexpressible, while Kafka created images of despair at transcending the limits of language.

One aspect of Hofmannsthal's response to skepticism about language was an evolution toward drama as his genre of preference. He published no more lyric poetry after the appearance of the *Chandos Brief* and explored the potential of drama to probe the ethical function of language as part of his increasingly central concern with "the social." Musil's generic preference likewise underwent a shift in the middle of his career, underscoring the significance of genre to an understanding of his work, and he, too, was motivated by ethical, as well as aesthetic, concerns. Generic form provides an opportunity for expression that does not presume natural correspondence between sign and object or perception. Musil asserted the inextricable link between form and substance in expression when he quoted the film critic Bela Balázs' statement that each artistic medium is "eine unersetzbare Ausdrucksmöglichkeit" (GW8 1149) and when he defined style as the exact working out of a thought (GW7 942). Musil's comments raise the question of the relation between outer and inner form in acts of expression, particularly with regard to external features of genre and the functional necessities giving rise to them.

The importance to Musil of expression and the forms it can and should take cannot be overestimated. In his works in many genres, his deliberate investigations into questions of style, and, of course, in his choice of a career as a writer, issues of expression occupy a central position. In a diary entry citing an essay by Emerson, Musil proclaims the need for expression and the urgency attached to it: "Der Mensch gehört nur halb sich selbst—die andere Hälfte ist Ausdruck. Denn alle Menschen verlangen in ihrer Seelennot nach Ausdruck" (T1 170). On the next page, in a passage to which he later added the designation "Tonka," he insists that the capacity for expression carries with it both power and knowledge: "Es sind die armen Mädchen, die nicht sprechen können. Die Rede ist nicht nur ein Machtmittel, sondern ein Sinn mehr zur Aufnahme der Welt. Siehe das Citat aus Emerson und darüber hinaus. Etwas gut ausdrücken ist mehr als es gut sehen" (T1 170). The struggle for adequate forms of expression is projected onto several of the narrators and protagonists in Musil's Novellen. Most particularly, it produces the narrative "Tonka," an artistic means for narrator and author to render an experience transcending the conventionally speakable—a "schmerzvolles Geheimnis," to echo Emerson. Likewise, the narrator of "Die Amsel" struggles to express the "mystery" of past experiences by giving them form, and his attempt falls short as they fail to cohere into a whole and to provide a basis for ethical response.

Musil joined his contemporaries in perceiving verbal expression as precarious. Since words lack clear and singular meanings, he wrote in the first book of his journal, they are best avoided: "Allein alle Worte haben soviel Nebensinn, Doppelsinn, Nebenempfindung, Doppelempfindung, daß man gut thut sich von ihnen fern zu halten" (T1 2). He despairs at the impossibility of original expression, of capturing thought or experience that is not tainted by previous usage or distorted by syntactical strictures:

> Zwei Jahrtausende schreiben mit uns. Am meisten aber unsere Eltern und Großeltern. Punkt und Strichpunkt sind Rückschrittssymptome—Stillstandssymptome....
> Punkt und Strichpunkt machen wir nicht nur, weil wir es so lernten, sondern weil wir so denken.—Das ist daran das Gefährliche. Solange man in Sätzen mit Endpunkt denkt, lassen sich gewisse Dinge nicht sagen—höchstens vage fühlen. (T1 52f)

He continues by expressing the hope for a form of expression that would allow certain perspectives still lying on the threshold of consciousness to become clear and understandable. The paradigmatic force of the Novelle seems to have held out the possibility of counteracting the stagnation of overpunctuated language.

The importance Musil attached to the Novelle, as will be seen, derives in part from *Gestalt* theory, the view that language achieves meaning in relation, that is, at the formal level of sentence and work rather than at the lexical (or semiotic) level of word (or sign). In combinations and relationships, in ever changing contexts rather than in isolated correspondences to referents, words mean. The task of the artist is to render experience in forms that reveal truths and compel responses that are more authentic than the habitual reactions provoked by encrusted, outworn forms: "Stilisiren heißt sehen u sehen lehren" (T2 813), and later, "Soweit Kunst Abstraktion ist, ist sie schon dadurch auch Zusammenfassung zu einem neuen Zusammenhang" (GW8 1139). These comments underscore Musil's concern with the power of form to compel response that becomes a central concern of his engagement with literature.

Musil's concept of "stilisiren"—stylizing as forming and re-forming—as an aesthetic means of seeing and teaching to see anticipates almost twenty years earlier the concept of "defamiliarization" put forth in 1917 by Victor Shklovsky in his essay "Art as Technique." Like Musil, Shklovsky criticized the inclination to perceive objects unconsciously, in forms so worn as to be unnoticeable. An object perceived in this "algebraic" mode of thought, which Shklovsky associates with prose, "fades and does not leave even a first impression; ultimately even the essence of what it was is forgotten."[22] Poetic language, Shklovsky argues, augments perception by "creating the strongest possible impression" (Shklovsky 8). Art is a means of countering flatness of experience: "And art exists that one may recover the sensation of life; it exists to make one feel things, to make the stone stony. The purpose of art is to impart the sensation of things as they are perceived and not as they are known. The technique of art is to make objects 'unfamiliar,' to make forms difficult, to increase the difficulty and length of perception because the process of perception is an esthetic end in itself and must be prolonged. Art is a way of experiencing the artfulness of an object; the object is not important" (Shklovsky 12). Musil's technique—creating new forms and constellations that call attention to as yet unperceived dimensions of experience and thus evoking a unique and forceful response—bears similarity to Shklovsky's "defamiliarization."

Though Shklovsky indicates that art enhances perception of objects by constructing a new image of them, Musil's view of language as "ein Sinn mehr zur Aufnahme der Welt," indicates a firmer bond between language and reality, between art and knowledge, than Shklovsky asserts. Musil refuses to grant a radical distinction between experience of an object and knowledge of it. The object *is*, in his eyes, important. He would agree with Shklovsky that literature mediates experience, but he maintains that it mediates knowledge by doing so: "Indem die Dichtung Erlebnis vermittelt, vermittelt sie Erkenntnis" (GW8 1224). While rejecting a purely aesthetic view of literature, Musil does qualify his concept of knowledge in continuing: "diese Erkenntnis ist zwar durchaus nicht die rationale der Wahrheit (wenn sie auch mit ihr vermengt ist), aber beide sind das Ergebnis gleichgerichteter Vorgänge, da es ja auch nicht eine rationale Welt und außer ihr eine irrationale, sondern nur eine Welt gibt, die beides enthält" (GW8 1224).

Shklovsky's qualification raises an issue addressed by another of the Russian Formalists, Roman Jakobson—the relation between technique and object of portrayal in literature. In his essay "On Realism in Art," Jakobson calls attention to the confusion of method and object in most discussions of "realism." Though realism is generally understood as "an artistic trend which aims at conveying reality as closely as possible,"[23] controversy about what is "realistic" most often stems from disagreement about narrative technique. Whether technique falls within the limits of a given artistic tradition that is perceived as faithfulness to reality, or whether, as with avant-garde art, it deforms the realistic code in order to render reality more accurately, whether, in Musil's terms, it holds to formulaic modes of expression or transcends them, the goal of illuminating something beyond the text is a goal common to Musil and the Russian Formalists.

The issue of realism leads back to one of the central concerns of Novelle theory, the tension between objectivity and subjectivity and the claim to exemplify truth about experience. Objectivity or realism, as in Goethe's demand that the novellistic event have occurred ("sich ereignet") and A. W. Schlegel's requirement that it meet the conditions of reality, are set against the subjective molding of the narrative such that it mediates a subjective vision of the "truth" of an unusual event. Jakobson's acknowledgment of the tension within the concept of realism and Musil's declaration of the connection between experience and knowledge in literature raise the question addressed in the next chapter of the interaction between mimetic and mythic impulses in the Novellen of *Vereinigungen* and *Drei Frauen*.

NOTES

1. Wilfried Berghahn, *Robert Musil* (Hamburg: Rowohlt, 1963).

2. Ingo Seidler, "Das Nietzschebild Robert Musils," *Nietzsche und die deutsche Literatur*, ed. Bruno Hillebrand (Tübingen: Niemeyer, 1978) 164.

3. Aldo Venturelli, "Die Kunst als fröhliche Wissenschaft: Zum Verhältnis Musils zu Nietzsche," *Nietzsche-Studien* 9 (1980) 302f.

4. Friedrich Nietzsche, *Jenseits von Gut und Böse*, Werke 6.2 hrsg. Giorgio Colli und Mazzino Montinari, (Berlin: de Gruyter, 1968) 149f.

5. In addition to the articles by Venturelli and Seidler, I have benefited from insights into Nietzschean thought presented in lectures by Walter H. Sokel at the University of Virginia in the winter of 1980.

6. Seidler, 174.

7. Peter Berger, "Robert Musil and the Salvage of the Self," *Partisan Review*, 51 (1984) 639-651.

8. See, for example, Claudia Monti, "Die Mach-Rezeption bei Hermann Bahr und Robert Musil," *Musil-Forum* 10 (1984) 201-213. The concept of "das unrettbare Ich" stems from Mach's *Analyse der Empfindungen*.

9. Though the following information on experimental and phenomenological psychology is culled from a variety of sources, it is derived in greatest measure from the comprehensive work of Edward G. Boring, *A History of Experimental Psychology* (New York: Appleton, Century, Crofts, 1949).

10. "Contents of consciousness" is the most common designation for Wundt's elements of experience. The phrase "true sensations" is from Wolfgang Köhler's book *Gestalt Psychology* (New York: Liveright, 1929).

11. Boring, 350.

12. Boring, 351.

13. Boring, 349.

14. *Encyclopedia of Philosophy*, ed. Paul Edwards (New York: Macmillan, 1967) 29.

15. Robert Musil, *Beiträge zur Beurteilung der Lehren Machs* (Hamburg: Rowohlt, 1980).

16. Boring, 433f.

17. Boring, 356.

18. David Luft, *Robert Musil and the Crisis of European Culture* (Berkeley: University of California Press, 1980) 68.

19. Köhler, 51f.

20. Köhler, 94.

21. Köhler, 204.

22. Victor Shklovsky, "Art as Technique," in: *Russian Formalist Criticism: Four Essays,* tr. Lee T. Lemon and Marion J. Reis (Lincoln: University of Nebraska Press, 1965) 11.

23. Roman Jakobson, "On Realism in Art," in: *Readings in Russian Poetics: Formalist and Structuralist Views,* ed. Ladislav Matejka and Krystyna Pomorska (Cambridge: Harvard University Press, 1971) 38.

CHAPTER THREE

From Mimesis to Myth: *Vereinigungen* to *Drei Frauen*

The terms "mimesis" and "myth" appearing in Aristotle's *Poetics* mark the poles of a tension in literature that is distilled and highlighted in the compact form of the Novelle. Aristotle claimed that the impulse to imitate—mimesis—is an inherent human trait: [Man] "is distinguished among the animals by being the most imitative of them, and he takes the first steps of his education by imitating."[1] Art imitates action, according to Aristotle, and the highest poetic arts, tragedy and epic, imitate noble actions of heroic characters.

Mimetic representation is, however, necessarily structured, and Aristotle called this structure—"the way the incidents should be plotted"—*mythos* or fable. Myth is the form taken by an imitation, which exhibits unity, closure, size, and proportion. Unity derives not from the subject portrayed, Aristotle noted, not from taking one man for its subject, but rather from the design: ". . . the events of which it is made up must be so plotted that if any of these elements is moved or removed the whole is altered and upset" (28). Further, he asserted, "it is not the poet's business to tell what has happened, but the kind of things that would happen—what is possible according to probability or necessity" (29). Because "poetry universalizes more, whereas history particularizes" (29), a well-formed myth should reveal necessity and probability and transcend history, exhibiting a higher truth than does a record of particular, contingent events.

The interaction of subjective and objective tendencies asserted by Friedrich and August Wilhelm Schlegel as the fundamental structuring principle of the Novelle reiterates the Aristotelian linking of mimesis and myth. Though they interact in and inform all narrative, the condensation characteristic of the Novelle sets the structural tension caused by them in relief. The tension creates a conflict for Musil, emerging repeatedly in his theoretical statements, particularly those written as he worked on his first two Novellen.

The other aspect of the Novelle recognized in the practical and critical tradition, its exemplary function or "claim to truth," implicitly takes up the mythic dimension of verbal art set forth in the Poetics, the transcendence through plot of the particulars of story or history (mimetic content) toward probability or necessity. Because both these aspects of myth—structure and expression of "truth"—have emerged as focal points in the tradition of the Novelle, they bear consideration as a key to the specific character of this genre within Musil's fiction. They will be examined in Musil's narratives as they interact with the mimetic component, the implicit claim to represent objects and actions in the "real" world of matter and sense.

In a study entitled *The Narrative of Realism and Myth*, Gregory Lucente affirms the "requisite interaction" of realistic and mythical elements in prose fiction.[2] Narrative discourse, he writes, while taking "those elements that claim a clear and definite position in space and time (and so in culture) as its subject matter, structures that material according to preexistent schematic categories." He argues that principles of selection and ordering and of spatial and temporal structure betray ideological (subjective) motivations even within the "realistic" text (44). The principles of ordering and selection are subjectively motivated and permit subjective control of discourse because ideologically motivated categories can be imposed on a narrative that appears to represent objective, realistic events. This ideological, mythic factor can be seen, for instance, in a painting in which a natural scene is selected and rendered so as to illustrate an idea or ideal, a divine presence, for example, as well as to depict a specific landscape. Literary objects and characters, too, however "true to life" they may be, often carry subjectively charged meaning.

Representation of objects and events in the sensible world was the characteristic goal of the literary realism of the nineteenth century. The novel, by virtue of its breadth and attention to detail, was viewed as the genre best suited to capturing the fullness of the natural and social world, but the Novelle, too, had been held by its theorists to the task of faithfully portraying external reality—"das Locale und das Costüm," as Friedrich Schlegel wrote, or the "täglichen Weltlauf," to speak with his brother. Subjective control and formal manipulation, ultimately the basis of the genre, were to be "concealed" in objective cover. (F. Schlegel used "verhüllt" and "verborgen," words echoed a century later in G. Lukács' "verstecken."[3]) Though a "subjektive Stimmung und Ansicht" (F. Schlegel) were to constitute the core of the Novelle, its subject matter was to be a realistic, though unusual, occurrence. The narrative task was mediation of the occurrence to a community whose expectations prevented assimilation of the improbable. Two "objective" spheres confront the narrator and each other in the Novelle—a realistic event, apparently independent of subjective fantasy or will, and the ordered understanding of a general community. As discussed in the previous chapter, the (necessarily) subjective narrator mediates between these spheres.

The task of mediation accomplished in and through the Novelle entails the interplay of mimesis and myth. Though these poetic impulses coexist in all narrative, the tension between them is especially crucial to the Novelle, which accentuates that tension and treats it in part as its subject matter. Moreover, the mimetic and mythic tasks vied for predominance in Musil's fiction, creating a conflict which attained a variety of resolutions in his six No-vellen. Through the Novelle Musil synthesized two primary but opposing concerns: In his scientific pursuit of knowledge, he attempted to record, to "capture," facts in the world of concrete objects and practical actions. He saw the role of art in this pursuit as a means of obtaining and imparting knowledge aesthetically, by making it "fühlbar" rather than "begreiflich."[4] At the same time, as a creative writer, he sought to transcend the limits of empirical observation and scientific description by em-bedding these in fictional discourse, a mythical structure that explains, interprets, and accords value to facts as it renders them.

The impulse toward myth-making—structuring, designing, plotting—reveals itself on several levels in Musil's Novellen. Its most evident manifestation is in common figural language. Images of delineating and defining space—one sense of plotting—recur throughout the works in metaphors of surface areas (*Fläche, Meer, Spiegel, Garten*), circles, architectural structures (houses, rooms, arches, vaults), lines, and borders. The desire to define and design space demonstrated in the thematic content reflects the attempt to construct meaning through form.

Further evidence of the importance of myth to the Novellen is the choice of genre itself. The Novellen are structured as paradigms, designed to bear the quality of *exemplum* traditionally attributed to the genre, but in a modern variation. Musil's Novellen depict realistic facts but plot them in a way that betrays subjective influence, not, however, in order to call attention to the limitations of "mere" fictionality but rather to claim exemplary validity. Musil's adaptation of the traditional notion of the *exemplum* offers him the opportunity to forge the link between aesthetic and ethical achievement that he declared central to his literary accomplishment. The interaction of mimesis and myth in his Novellen sheds light on the significance of the genre for Musil, and also on his role in its history, particularly its adaptation to an era inhospitable to closure and apodictic ambitions.

Despite initial impressions to the contrary, the *Vereinigungen*, Musil's first two Novellen, published in 1911, are his most consistently mimetic, realistic, attempts in the genre. Readers' difficulty with them and public reaction against their unorthodox style notwithstanding, they represent an attempt to imitate in the medium of language phenomena from the "real" world. The inner world and sensual experience that they portray would not have qualified as "real" for the Schlegels and their contemporaries in the early nineteenth century, but it was accorded reality by Musil and his contemporaries at the turn to the twentieth century. Interest in the sensual realm had become a logical extension of earlier efforts of natural scientists to observe and record material reality, while writers had sought to represent it in works of literature. At the turn of the century interest in the "real" persisted but had been redefined, broadened to include the inner reality that was the subject of the burgeoning field of psychology. As we have seen, this development was taken so far by some psychologists and philosophers that sensations were proposed as the *only* facts to be accepted as "real."

Musil shared the goal of the natural sciences—to know and understand the world, including human nature—and he asserted confidence that knowledge of reality beyond sensual elements and explanation of the forces governing them was possible. Moreover, I will argue, Musil sought to convey such knowledge in his Novellen, a task he viewed as problematic but not impossible. His doubts about the capacity of language led him to expand, rather than deny, its communicative force.

In a diary entry of 1911, written as he was working on the *Vereinigungen*, Musil expressed a desire to complete the unfinished business of Naturalism, which had as its goal the knowledge of nature, in this specific case of a human psyche. He asserted confidence in literature to represent its object while also revealing awareness of the difficulty of such an endeavor:

> Naturalismus: In Erinnerungen meiner ersten Ein-
> drücke von moderner Literatur will mir dieses Wort
> immer noch als ein niemals eingelöstes Versprechen
> erscheinen....Man zeichne nun auf, was ein...im
> realen Leben als einheitlich empfundener Mensch
> denkt u spricht. Es wirkt total   uneinheitlich....Das
> nun anders zu tun, dabei irgendwie liegt der
> problematische Naturalismus...Es erscheint mir
> nicht ausgeschlossen, daß ein vollkommen adäqua-
> tes Register der Gedanken eines ganzen Lebens...
> scheinbar einheitslos wie es ist, von erschütternder
> Kunstwirkung wäre. Aber es ist eine physische
> Unmöglichkeit, es ist eben etwas, das man nie
> wirklich versuchen kann. Doch kann man an solche
> Möglichkeiten denken u. Wirkungen suchen, die sich
> ihnen, sogut es uns gegeben ist, annähern. (T1 117)

In order to provide a register of mental activity without reducing it, Musil took measures of the sort later held by Roman Jakobson to mark the revolutionary artist. Adopting a strategy misunderstood by the conservative public as a distortion of reality,[5] he   deformed existing artistic canons in order to more closely and effectively imitate that reality.

Musil responded to the challenge of "problematic Naturalism" with the *Vereinigungen*. Despite the unconventional style of these Novellen, a mimetic claim to reflect an extratextual reality prevails over subjective, mythic structuration more than in the later Novellen. The *Vereinigungen* are in effect phenomenological case studies in literary form. The voice that speaks them is that of a narrator who remains distinct from the figures. In probing sensations and psychic processes, the narrator often adopts a point of view close to that of the characters, but he remains distinct from them as would a scientific observer. The narrator assumes a posture like that of a clinical psychologist employing the phenomenological method of observing and recording the direct experience of a patient. Not restricting observation to behavioral responses alone, as would a physiological psychologist or behaviorist, the phenomenological psychologist relies on self-report of direct experience. He thus allows a subjective element to color his findings, in fact welcoming that subjective coloration as an important ingredient of the experience he is studying, while also demanding a high degree of precision in identifying and recording the experience reported by the subject. Placing a mind under the microscope, as it were, the narrator probes deeply but focalizes his vision through the character.

The narrator must, of course, employ the synthetic operations of language to record and communicate the perceptual activity he observes, including that which remains subverbal for the character. As with other scientific techniques for recording and synthesizing information, the narrator's command over language does not indicate full authorial knowledge of the characters' experience or control over them. Rather, the language employed by the narrator—frequent use of analogies rather than direct statement, conjecture and comparison expressed in the subjunctive mode, and recurring adverbs of uncertainty such as "vielleicht" and "irgend"—attains a high degree of precision in recording the complex processes of perception/reflection. It permits expression of experience not readily able to fit the molds of established scientific categories, and it also acknowledges the limitations of the observer/narrator, some of which he may share with the subjects/characters whose experience and perception occupies him.

Musil wrote that he had decided to follow "den 'maximal belasteten Weg' ...den Weg des allmählichsten, unmerklichsten Übergangs" (GW7 972) in the *Vereinigungen*. All his Novellen contain dense descriptions of inner and outer worlds, reports of action and reflections on it, anticipation of future consequences or possibilities, and analogies that express minute details and subtle aspects of psychic activity with great richness and refinement, while eschewing the measurable accuracy (with its attendant limitations) of a distanced, behaviorist, "objective" approach. These minutely sensitive—and thus mimetic—narrative techniques expand the proportion of time of narration to narrated time, swelling the discourse and slowing down the tempo. Most particularly, the analogies fuse narrator's and figure's perspectives, as Dorrit Cohn has explained insightfully,[6] allowing portrayal of states of mind that have not attained the level of consciousness required for verbal articulation. Though the distinction between the psychic events of the story and the narrator's discourse cannot easily be drawn, the goal indicated by the narrative is nonetheless naturalistic representation of phenomena external to the literary work.

The inner reality represented in Musil's *Vereinigungen* is every bit as "realistic" as the objective reality deemed by the Schlegels to be the province of the Novelle. These works therefore participate in the traditional enterprise of the Novelle—mediation of a fact to an audience to whom it is otherwise surprising, indeed disturbing. For Musil's contemporaries in a time of rising awareness of the vast possibilities and power of the psyche, and especially of the role of sexuality in both conscious and unconscious thought processes, an unexpected inner tremor required mediation as urgently as did Kleist's earthquake or the supernatural forces disrupting the fictional worlds of E. T. A. Hoffmann's characters.

In Musil's Novellen, thoughts are the events; despite their inwardness they occur independently of subjective control. Musil acknowledges the independent reality of psychic events when he writes, "Der Gedanke ist nicht etwas das ein innerlich Geschehenes betrachtet sondern er ist dieses innerlich Geschehene selbst./ Wir denken nicht über etwas nach, sondern etwas denkt sich in uns herauf" (T1 117). The *Vereinigungen* portray thoughts and perceptions as events. At the same time a Novelle is, in Musil's eyes, an event, a "tremor" in itself, something "das über [den Dichter] hereinbricht, eine Erschütterung" (GW9 1465). The Novellen present themselves as representation of an event (the novellistic "Begebenheit") and as event itself (an act of mediation). The meaning of the works is a function of the relationship between the two levels.

The attempt to depict mental and sensual processes, Musil's mimetic intent, necessarily led him away from conventional realistic techniques, a shift that engages the author's attention, often verging on despair, as recorded in his journal (T1 213-250). Attention to sensations and perceptions rendered the convention of logical, linear narration inadequate to portray the "facts" as observed. Whereas the mind often operates by intuitive association rather than logical consequence, realistic narrative draws on rational rhetorical structures employed by the conscious mind engaged in cognitive thought.

Conventional realistic discourse, however, reliant on principles such as causality and chronology, imposes systematic constraints on psychic activity. The raw data of perception elude systematic categories and must be distorted to fit the structures of language. In the *Vereinigungen* Musil pursues the empiricist's goal of observing and recording psychic phenomena without distortion. Formulating the conceptual design for the earlier version of "Versuchung der stillen Veronika" entitled "Das verzauberte Haus," (1908) Musil wrote: "Man sucht Ausdruck für neue inner Dinge, verzichtet aber ganz darauf, sie in einen Causalzusammenhang einzureihen. Man gibt eine Kette von Stimmungen, die ein Kontinuum u. dadurch den Teil eines Causalzusammenhanges bilden. Gewissermaßen seinen emotionalen Teil.... Man zeigt nur einen emotionalen, einen Stimmungsablauf, unter dem gerade noch hinreichend u. von selbst sich der Schein eines causalen Gefüges bildet" (GW8 1311). The beginning of each of the *Vereinigungen* can be seen as establishing a frame, though not in the explicit form of many nineteenth-century Novellen. The opening paragraphs or pages raise an issue that is then addressed in the subsequent narrative. The actions of the protagonist and her perceptions of and reflections on them form a paradigm, rather than a discursive analysis, in answer to the questions raised by the frame.

The initial scene of "Vollendung der Liebe," for example, erects a frame for the ensuing narrative, though the frame is more thematic than structural, never closing at the end. The position of Claudine and her husband relative to each other actually forms part of a frame, a "starren, steifen Winkel" (GW6 156). The scene has a static quality much like a daguerreotype; the couple is described as bound in an "Einheit, die man fast mit den

Sinnen spüren konnte," connected by a "Strebe aus härtestem Metall" (156). They are discussing G., a character in a book they have read, who has committed a violent sexual crime. The fictional case incites a process of questioning in Claudine. She voices her disturbance to her husband in the "frame" and her uncertainties occupy her during her journey. The fictional story of G. thus functions as a catalyst, setting thoughts and actions in motion which in turn become the story recounted in the ensuing narrative.

Two main questions occupy Claudine: the relation of intention to behavior and its ethical import, and the status of the self as either essentially isolated and independent or bound to and defined by another person. In the discussion with her husband she ties the issue of intention to the possibility of union with another when she deliberates the moral question of G.'s guilt: "Ich glaube, er meint gut zu handeln" (158) followed soon thereafter by the query, "Ist nicht jedes Gehirn etwas Einsames und Alleiniges?" (159). During her three-day journey and separation from her husband, she commits adultery with a stranger, incurring guilt as judged from a conventional, external standpoint, and yet gaining the "perfection of love," an intense, subjectively sensed union with her husband together with a heightened awareness of her own individual existence. The experience and the import she accords it derive from her subjective stance, her own perception, interpretation, and evaluation of her action. The story of her journey provides fictional elaboration on the questions raised in connection with G. at the beginning of the Novelle. Instead of presenting the problem discursively, the narrator designs a plot; rather than analyzing motives and actions, he creates a parabolic image of the "irgendwas Bestimmtem, das für [Claudine] bereits hinter [G.] dämmerte"(157), the vague sense of deeper significance that Claudine feels but does not articulate.

In a similar fashion the beginning of "Versuchung der stillen Veronika," establishes a frame for the ensuing narrative. In this case it is the opening paragraph that forms the frame. Instead of depicting a scene as in "Vollendung der Liebe," it directs a rather abstract injunction to the audience to imagine or allow the narrative situation: "Irgendwo muß man zwei Stimmen hören" (GW6 194). The imperative "must" suspends the question of motivation that had bothered Musil in conceiving the Novelle (T1 220f). Collapsing the distinction between listening and reading, the narrator asserts that the listener/reader should discern voices as if they were lying on a page or projected like beams that might converge at a point in space. The reader thus should share the task of the narrator attending to the characters as a clinical psychologist would attend to a subject's report of experience.

The purpose of the process of observation suggested by the final sentence of the paragraph adds a value-giving dimension to the empirical task: "Vielleicht, daß diese Stücke hier dann aneinander sprängen, aus ihrer Krankheit und Schwäche hinweg ins Klare, Tagfeste, Aufgerichtete" (GW6 194). Listening, and by implication narrating/recording, might draw out that which is unclear, weak, even sick, and endow it with form—visibility, stability, and stature. Narrator and reader together should define, clarify, and, in effect, heal the raw and vague sensations of the character and perhaps of the mediating observer as well. Therapeutic and aesthetic value are thus accorded to the mythic-mimetic process, the representation of "zwei Stimmen" in a narrative plot with an implied spatial dimension, and the act of reception that completes it. Narrative conveys knowledge and functions as a means of healing.

The challenge presented by the narrative situation is reflected in the characters' struggle to articulate their thoughts and to know and understand those of their companions. Representation and interpretive response, which together constitute the act of communication, assume thereby thematic, as well as stylistic, significance in the Novellen; they inform the story as well as the discourse in which it is embedded. Veronika's and Johannes' efforts to convey their perceptions to each other, and Claudine's wonder at discovering thoughts and emotions in herself that remain inaccessible to her husband, raise the issue of communicability and reflect the narrator's task of probing the psyche and formulating his findings in language. The characters' difficulties in understanding one another in turn call attention to the issue of reception and interpretation, of the reader's challenge to make sense of the text.

The temporal structure of the *Vereinigungen* departs from conventional realism, but it does so in order to remain "true to life" where the conventional chronological time structure of a realistic plot falls short of this, its goal. The retardation of the narrative time (*Erzählzeit*), achieved by the abundance of descriptive detail, analogies, and conjectures, actually brings it into closer alignment with the narrated time (*erzählte Zeit*), the time of the action, that is, in these texts, of the characters' thoughts.[7] The total submersion of narrative time into the time of the story, impossible to achieve, would be the ideal of Naturalism—the distortion of representation would be eliminated. In the *Vereinigungen*, distortion does occur when the narrative time—the time required to articulate mental processes—exceeds the time required for the momentary sensations portrayed, and yet the temporal distortion renders the operations of the mind to a degree of fullness and subtlety unattained in the summarization common in earlier narrative prose. Especially in the case of Veronika, of whom we learn, "das Zeitmaß ihres Lebens war...ganz langsam" (GW6 207), the tempo of the expanded discourse represents its object far more adequately than a more concise formulation would. In addition, narration of characters' past memories and anticipation of future occurrences achieves greater mimetic accuracy than would chronologically ordered narrative in that it portrays the meshing of past and future into the present that is typical of the psyche. Again the technique entails innovative manipulation of language, often perceived as unrealistic, but the goal and effect—to represent nonfictional reality—remains that of a mimetic conception of art.

In journal entries written as he was completing the *Vereinigungen,* Musil addresses a conflict to which he sought solutions throughout his career and which he connects with the question of genre. The problem arises when he breaks with conventions of realism and attempts to portray "das Gebiet der Werte und Bewertungen, das der ethischen und aesthetischen Beziehungen, das Gebiet der Idee" (GW8 1028). He bemoans the result of his efforts in the *Vereinigungen,* which he calls, "Schöne Partien aber zu sehr Essay, aneinandergefädelte Betrachtungen, intellektuelle [Phantasien] Paraphrasen über den Vorwand eines Themas" (T1 213). His character Veronika, he writes, "spricht noch zu sehr um der Gedanken willen u. zu wenig aus der Situation heraus" (T1 213), more like a book (T1 220) than a person. As an antidote to this excess of philosophical reflection, Musil looks to the techniques of realism, which represent actions in the external world: "Drittens muß ich, was ich mir schon früher vornahm, etwas mehr im gemeinen Sinn erzählend sein, man darf nicht nur bei der Entwicklung eines inneren Prozeßes aus inneren Notwendigkeiten dabei sein, sondern man muß auch einen Menschen in Steigerungen aus einer Situation in die andere geraten sehen" (T1 214). Immediately thereafter, however, he admits the difficulty of carrying out this intention to locate motivation in the "situation" (empirical circumstances) of the characters rather than in "inner necessity" and reveals concern that theoretical discourse will overcome the mimetic rendering of actions, perhaps all the more so when the actions are internal (T1 214).

Musil raises the issue of genre again in connection with "Vollendung der Liebe": "Es darf in Claudine nicht heißen: irgendwo begann eine Uhr mit sich selbst zu sprechen, Schritte gingen, u.s.w.—Das ist Lyrik. Es muß heißen: eine Uhr schlug, Claudine empfand es als begänne irgendwo...Schritte gingen usw—Im ersten Fall sagt der Autor durch die Gewähltheit des Gleichnisses selbst wie schön, er betont das soll schön sein udgl" (T1 226). The epic form should, Musil asserts, describe characters and attribute thoughts and sensations to them. Otherwise, he implies, they lose their objectivity. The solution he proposes again harks back to realism:

> Maxime: Der Autor zeige sich nur *in den ministeriellen Bekleidungsstücken seiner Personen.* Er wälze immer die Verantwortung auf sie ab. Das ist nicht nur klüger sondern merkwürdigerweise *entsteht dadurch das Epische...*Es ist das, was mir unklar vorschwebte, als ich von Claudine schrieb, ich müsse hier mehr im gemeinen Sinn erzählend sein u. von Veronika notierte, *ich wolle nicht das Problem der Sodomie erläutern sondern nur erzählen, was sie darüber fühlt.* (T1 226; emphasis added)

As these reflections demonstrate, Musil was concerned with both subjective and objective poles of narrative: The author's philosophical (essayistic) ruminations and (lyrical) moods should be filtered through the figures. Musil cites the absence of point of view—lack of an identifiable subject—as "der technische Hauptfehler der bisherigen Fassung" of the *Vereinigungen* (T1 221). The objects of observation concern him also, as he strives to preserve "das

Epische": "Man muß einfach Geschichten erfinden, Dinge
erzählen, die sich in Tatsachen ausdrücken lassen, heute
dies morgen jenes, sich damit Zeit lassen...Dann das andere
hineinarbeiten" (T1 226). And he elaborates in a further
passage the importance of mimetic representation without
subjective intervention or control: "Man soll möglichst oft
Tatsachen aussprechen lassen statt Gefühle...D.h. also
Dinge, die Anspruch auf objektive Geltung haben, nicht
bloß auf subjektive" (T1 239). Musil thus looks to the
world—people, objects, events—for models for fiction.

Throughout the fifth notebook of his diary, Musil
wavers between adopting realistic techniques and
developing a different style that would accommodate his
philosophical interest in expressing abstract ideas ("die
Bedeutungen selbst" [GW8 1318], "das Gebiet der Idee"
[GW8 1028]). He dramatizes this self-conflict in a fictional diaogue entitled "Über Robert Musil's Bücher" (1913). A
narrator, a critic, and a writer discuss Musil's works,
specifically the conflict between mimetic realism and
theoretical discourse in fiction (GW8 996). The argument
pursues the conflict between the alleged need for mimetic
description of action, which the critic and the writer
defend, and the narrator's defense of the synthetic,
constructive purpose of literature. The piece places Musil's
persistent anxiety about excessive intellectualism on a
fictional stage. The narrator calls for a new development
in narrative in which "begriffsstarke Menschen" serve as
focal points for the depiction of reality. Seeking to retain
the mimetic principle of portraying reality through an
individual character in order to retain its singularity and
its emotional and intellectual significance, the narrator
demands: "...daß die Schilderung der Realität endlich
zum dienenden Mittel des begriffsstarken Menschen werde,
mit dessen Hilfe er sich an Gefühlserkenntnisse und
Denkerschütterungen heranschleicht, die allgemein und in

Begriffen nicht, sondern nur im Flimmern des Einzelfalls ... zu erfassen sind" (GW8 997).

Musil's emphasis on portraying "begriffsstarke Menschen" but not *Begriffe* themselves leads him, ironically, away from mimesis and toward mythic portrayal; it is in the Novelle especially, as we shall see in *Drei Frauen*, that he seeks to capture the "Flimmern des Einzelfalls" in a paradigm, a mythical image, rather than to elucidate a concept in theoretical discourse or "das Erzählen einfach eines starken begriffsarmen Menschen."

The focus on thinking (begriffsstarke) characters and their insights, however, as the critic quickly points out to the narrator of the sketch, poses a threat to *Lebendigkeit*, the dynamic quality of great fiction. The writer's task is *schildern*, descriptive portrayal (GW8 997f); according to the critic, Musil fails to live up to the task. The young writer adds to this criticism the fear that literature born of Musil's ambitions forfeits its connection to cultural and historical reality: "Mag dem sein, wie es will, ... es ist Theorie, und eine solche, theoretisch ausgeklügelte Technik mag dem Wesen dieses Schriftstellers passen. Praktisch bestehen bleibt, was ich schon vorhin sagte, daß diese Bücher mit den wahrhaften Kräften unserer Zeit einfach nicht das geringste zu tun haben. Sie wenden sich an einen kleinen Kreis von Hypersensiblen, die keine Realitätsgefühle mehr—nicht einmal perverse—haben, sondern nur literarische Vorstellungen davon" (GW8 999). Musil's defender, the narrator, insists on a compromise, a new form of art that occupies a middle ground between conceptuality and concreteness. He holds that literature must convey the conceptual context of experience since experience acquires meaning only in dialectical exchange with interpretation: "Wo uns ein Mensch erschüttert und beeinflußt, geschieht es dadurch, daß sich uns die Gedankengruppen eröffnen, unter denen er seine Erlebnisse zusammenfaßt, und die Gefühle, wie sie in dieser komplizierten wechselwirkenden Synthese eine überraschende Bedeutung gewinnen" (GW8 1001). And yet, despite the apparent assurance of this defense, the stylistic conflict between mimetic portrayal and philosophical discourse, and the generic one between epic and essay, continued to plague Musil. Even as he wrote *Mann ohne Eigenschaften,* he expressed anxiety, "daß dabei etwas herauskommt, das nicht Fleisch und nicht Fisch ist."[8] For a time, however, he turned to the genre Novelle to give form to ideas.

When Musil did depart from realism, from mimetic representation of psychic activity, several paths were open to him. One major route led to the essays; *Mann ohne Eigenschaften* was the result of another. In the novel he attempted to synthesize essayistic and epic structures, relying heavily on irony to mesh the two genres and convey meaning. The Novellen, on the other hand, offered possibilities for narrative beyond simple storytelling while also avoiding theoretical intrusion. They were a product of Musil's exhortation to himself in a foreword to the *Vereinigungen*: "Bilde Dichter, rede nicht! Gegen diese Forderung wird hier zu sehr verstoßen" (GW8 1312). Through the process of "bilden," Musil uses the "ministerielle Bekleidungsstücke" of his characters, a principle he drew from realism, as cloaks for ideas; in actuality, however, this technique led in the opposite direction from the poetics of mimesis and issued in a distinctive type of modern myth.

Several features of *Drei Frauen* (1924) offer evidence that Musil sought refuge in realistic techniques, as he had indicated in his diary that he would, in order to avoid "reden"—reflective, essayistic, potentially "hypersensitive" esoteric narrative. Fairly clear, easily paraphraseable actions in an identifiable world of objects and characters structure these Novellen. "Die Portugiesin" begins, as might any realistic narrative of the nineteenth century, with details of the family history of the protagonist and description of the setting. The reference to historical chronicles (*Urkunden*) adds to the tone of realistic accuracy. "Grigia" features detailed description of natural surroundings, taken in great part from Musil's diary entries describing his environs and experiences during World War I. And the portrayal of the urban milieu in "Tonka" and later "Die Amsel" indicate a return to the conventional realistic dictum to represent material, social, and historical reality.

Upon closer examination, however, the reader becomes aware that in the case of each of these ficitonal worlds, "Es war eine Welt, die eigentlich keine Welt war" (GW6 255), as the narrator of "Die Portugiesin" states of the territory surrounding the Ketten castle. What Musil has in fact created, especially in "Grigia" and "Die Portugiesin," are mythical worlds designed to give form to ideas—to follow the directive, "Bilde, Dichter. Rede nicht!" (GW8 1312). These Novellen likewise comply with Johannes' wish in "Versuchung der stillen Veronika," that the vague but powerful force within him take on tangible form: "'Kreisendes,' flehte Johannes, 'daß du ein Kleid hättest, an dessen Falten ich dich halten könnte. Daß ich mit dir sprechen könnte. Daß ich sagen könnte: du bist Gott, und ein kleines Steinchen unter der Zunge trüge, wenn ich von dir rede, um der größeren Wirklichkeit willen! Daß ich sagen könnte: dir befehle ich mich, du wirst mir helfen, du siehst mir zu, mag ich tun was ich will, etwas von mir liegt reglos und mittelpunktsstill, und das bist du'" (GW6 194f). In expressing the desire to touch the irrational force that he senses, to find it embodied in tangible, plastic form, Johannes' wish anticipates Musil's strategy, carried out in *Drei Frauen*, of cloaking philosophical ideas and emotions in fictional *Bekleidungsstücke*, thus creating an illusory appearance of realism. In "Grigia" and "Die Portugiesin," the fictional world and the characters who inhabit it, especially the titular women, embody needs and desires of the male protagonists. The inner world turns outward and the object of the protagonist's metaphysical yearning suddenly takes on human form and wears a dress, "an dessen Falten [er sich] halten könnte."

Rather than representing actual women inhabiting a real, mundane universe, the female figures in this volume all are embodiments of ideas, most of which are associated with the unreal and nonrational. In Homo's eyes his wife becomes a partner in a mystical union that transcends his physical, earthy, relationship to Grigia. Grigia, in turn, embodies for him a primitive, natural life free of the constraints of the society he has left behind. Ketten sees in the Portugiesin the exotic, "das andere"—the magical, uncanny, daemonic, or divine. And Tonka, who becomes in the mind of her scientific, rational friend a sacrificial victim and savior, is characterized by the narrator as "...Natur, die sich zum Geist ordnet" (GW6 285). The schematic opposition of the female characters to the rational, mundane world, to "das Locale und das Costüm," signals, in contrast to the initial impression of realism, a move in *Drei Frauen* away from the mimetic enterprise of the *Vereinigungen* toward a poetics of myth.

Despite its context in diary entries expressing Musil's distress at the lack of realism in *Vereinigungen*, the exhortation, "Bilde, Dichter, rede nicht!" actually signals a retreat from realistic convention, and a Nietzschean embrace of creativity, artistry, and artifice—the myth-making capability in man. Musil assumes the task set forth by Nietzsche of creating new values by constructing new forms (*bilden*), creating fictions, rather than by conceptual discourse (*reden*) with its danger of petrifaction.

Extramoral in the Nietzschean sense of transcending moral codes, fiction can also, in Musil's view, fulfill an ethical purpose in that it teaches by example. Like myth in its function in primitive societies, fiction expresses "truth" through narrative, not by referring to an original or ultimate order but by creating the myth itself. In this concept, the two aspects of myth discussed by Aristotle are joined. "Myth" refers to narrative structure and to the transcendence of mimetic content as well.

In *Drei Frauen* this dimension of myth, the transcendence of mimetic content, like the Nietzschean ethical precept of fiction as extramoral, constructive lie, converges with the view of the Novelle as *exemplum* to produce a modern parable. Rather than teaching a specific lesson, as had its precursors in the Bible or the eighteenth-century moral tale or fable, Musil's modern parable points beyond a particular moral to a new constellation, an "unheard-of" situation, and draws from that a new ethos. Musil's Novellen present an otherwise inexpressible idea in condensed, symbolic form, though no overarching dogma or moral code grounds their interpretation.

Musil uses the genre Novelle to create a paradigm that "deutet an und schränkt ein" in contrast to the novel, which "sagt aus und sagt alles."[9] The paradigmatic force of the Novelle—the force of myth—is grasped both emotionally and rationally, thus combining both aspects of the psyche, *Seele* and *Verstand*, affective and rational faculties, that Musil sought to integrate in the quest for knowledge. Refusing, as Nietzsche had, to accept a radical distinction between science and art, Musil created Novellen as modern parables or "lies" serving a higher truth (like those told by Claudine and Agathe), fictions supplementing the rational means to truth.

Lucente's book on the interaction of realistic and mythical elements in narrative, discussed above, examines structures in apparently realistic (mimetic) prose that betray a mythical quality. Organization according to "pre-existent schematic categories" (44) betrays mythical (ideological) principles that shape a narrative and override its representative (mimetic) function. The

Novellen in the volume *Drei Frauen* reveal many such
constructs with sources outside historical or objective
reality, the abundance of which indicates a shift in
Musil's poetics away from the mimetic and toward the
mythical pole as he moved from his first to his second
volume of Novellen. Although the earlier *Vereinigungen*
display some mythical elements, the Novellen of *Drei
Frauen* represent the apex of the mythic phase in Musil's
literary production. The following schematic structures,
which emerge already in *Vereinigungen*, pervade the
works of this volume, most particularly "Grigia" and "Die
Portugiesin": 1) geometric forms, especially circles, in two
and three dimensions and in motion, associated with states
of mind and, more generally, with the self; 2) dichotomies,
patterns of binary opposition; 3) a structure of narcissism
that emerges from the conjunction of the circular structure
and the pattern of opposition; and 4) structures from older,
familiar myths.

The settings of "Grigia" and "Die Portugiesin" have
circular structures. The schematic nature of their fictional
worlds is accentuated by their hermetic isolation; the
secluded mountain valley to which Homo withdraws and
the castle of the Kettens are cut off from recognizably
realistic surroundings. The landscape around the village in
"Grigia," for example is described as shaped like an
empty Bundt pan. The narrator tells us it "...bestand aus
einem mehr als halbkreisförmigen Wall hoher...Berge,
welche steil zu einer Senkung abfielen, die rund um einen in
der Mitte stehenden kleineren und bewaldeten Kegel lief,
wodurch das Ganze einer leeren, gugelhupfförmigen Welt
ähnelte..."(236). The castle of the Kettens in "Die Portugiesin" also occupies the center of a circular landscape,
appearing to the foreign woman as she approaches it for
the first time, "als ritte man in einen großen zerborstenen
Topf hinein, der eine fremde grüne Farbe enthielt" (255).
Space and time merge in this unreal world, which is

"wochenweit und -tief" (255) and cut off from its surroundings by a series of walls, presumably rippling out from the inner circle, over which reputedly no one has ever succeeded in looking. The narrator explicitly identifies the setting as as a mythical landscape when he calls it "eine Welt, die eigentlich keine Welt war" (255).

The Portugiesin associates the castle and surrounding territory with her husband: "Oft hatte sie sich in Träumen dieses Land, aus dem der Mann kam, den sie liebte, nach seinem eigenen Wesen vorgestellt und das Wesen dieses Mannes nach dem, was er ihr von seiner Heimat erzählte" (255). The narrator also draws an analogy between Ketten and the castle in saying, "seine Heimat lag damals fern, sein wahres Wesen war etwas, auf das man wochenlang zureiten konnte, ohne es zu erreichen" (258). The world around the castle, then, despite the detailed description initially creating an impression of traditional realistic narrative, takes on a symbolic function by association with Ketten's "true being," the remote "something" always approached but never reached.

Other circular structures inform *Drei Frauen*, and in a less prominent way, the *Vereinigungen*. The circular shape of their setting is connected in some way with the attempt on the part of their main characters to circumscribe territory that would define a space associated with the "self" or at least an orientation point from which to interact with the world. Ketten, for example, discovers that his enemy, the bishop, occupies a personal territory, in which he lies on clean linen, surrounded by clerics and artists in his service, while Ketten *circles him like a wolf* (GW6 258). Having espied such accoutrements of social and personal identity, Ketten decides that he should furnish his own domain in a similar manner to the same end. He hires chaplain, scribe, maid, and cook and orders costly tapestries and other furnishings in a weak attempt to create a court society that might rival the bishop's. He himself, however, remains far from his "court," continuing to encircle the enemy with an aim to acquiring ever more territory and status for himself and the family chain (*Kette*) in which he occupies one link.

In "Vollendung der Liebe" Claudine associates circling with an intense perception of her self. She imagines, for example, the vantage point of her companion as he gazes at her as that of the ".. Augen eines kreisenden Vogels" (GW6 192), and the vision brings a sense of order to her self-perception. In another instance her pain is compared to "ein feines kreisendes Singen in ihrem Kopf" that pulls her thoughts in the same "schwankendes Kreisen" (162) after it. And later she imagines inhabiting the personal living quarters of a stranger, and the thought of perceiving the world from this foreign space, of finding "von allen Seiten die Welt geschlossen und ruhig auch um diesen Mittelpunkt stehn..." (177), while alternately repelling and fascinating her, provides in the vision of circular space a potential locus of personal identity. In "Versuchung der stillen Veronika" Johannes also imagines a *Mittelpunkt*, a central circular space around which the self can turn, when he yearns for a "Steinchen in einem Wirbel, das dir plötzlich den Mittelpunkt anzeigt, um den du dich drehst..." (202).

Claudine's memories of the years before her marriage and anticipation of an approaching erotic encounter appear to her as a circling of past, future, and present, "als dehnte sich plötzlich in ihr die unendliche Spannung ihrer Liebe weit über das Gegenwärtige in die Untreue hinaus, aus der sie einst zu ihnen beiden gekommen war wie aus einer früheren Form ihres ewigen Zwischenihnenseins" (174). She perceives her future as a return to her past, as "coming full circle," so to speak, with her marriage as the distance traveled in between. Like Ketten, who regains a measure of personal stability in scaling the wall to the castle, and A2, who finally returns to his childhood room and books, Claudine's life describes a circular route, plotting and defining her self.

The desire to define, describe, and delineate space in the Novellen alternates dialectically with the drive to dissolve and overcome boundaries. The tension between definition and dissolution engenders images of expansion and constriction, and of opening and closing, with a positive valuation resting at various times on one pole or the other. The assertion of force needed to break out of bounds and transcend limits, and, on the other hand, the energy concentrated into a constricted space to produce a "feeling of self" ("Gefühl von sich"), are produced by this tension, recalling the Nietzschean concept of energy produced by overcoming opposition.

The *Vereinigungen* contain many enclosed spaces defined by window frames, clothing, rooms, and houses. These spaces and structures carry out a mimetic function, but they assume symbolic significance as well. Several of these spatial planes and structures become the locus of a heightened sense of self for the characters, while others, Veronika's house for example, appear stagnant and confining, preventing self-awareness and -assertion. Some spatial images, in contrast, suggest expansiveness. The landscape outside Claudine's train, the sea, and the street, for example, offer release and a new frontier for the self, but just as suddenly incite the urge to draw inward and erect further boundaries around the self.[10]

These spatial images function as expressions of inner states and as "ideas" of the self cloaked in realistic, everyday form, that is, as mythic constructs of the self. The image they create of the self as a process of shaping, dissolving, and then reforming in a new context and from another perspective is one of greater coherence than the chaotic flux proclaimed by Bahr as replacing the self, and yet more dynamic and provisional than that of a given, stable entity developing organically and in accordance with laws of cause and effect.

Homo senses both constriction and dissolution as he separates from his family; he has a feeling of selfishness or self-dissolution (GW6 234)—he cannot decide which. Then, after entering the confines of the fairytale valley, he experiences an intense sense of union with his wife together with a feeling of release from his bond to life. Finally, he dies in the extreme confinement and isolation of a mine shaft.

Ketten, who "hatte sich aufgelöst wie ein Zug Wanderer" (262) during his sickness and senses an absence ("Ab-wesenheit") from himself, appears to overcome the threat of dissipation by climbing the wall and gaining entry into the castle and access to his wife. An impenetrable wall of rock and noise has erected a barrier around the pair, however, preserving, or even enforcing, their hermetic isolation.

The most significant schema structuring the fictional worlds of *Drei Frauen* is the bipolar opposition. There are many dichotomized pairs of values in these Novellen, and as is the case in much literature and thought at the turn of the century, they tend to be subsumed under the aegis of gender categories. On either side of the line dividing male and female stand opposing concepts including rational/nonrational, intellectual/sensual, active/passive, day/night, scientific/magical or religious, and hunter or warrior/gatherer.

Homo the generic "man" and Tonka's unnamed friend are representative types, professional scientists with a firm command of clear, rational language. They encounter lovers who speak (or sing) in unfamiliar, apparently unsystematic vocal sounds which they cannot comprehend. The *Herr* von Ketten (another generic man or lord with no given name) is a warrior, a man of intelligence and action. His wife, on the other hand, reads and speaks a

Zeichensprache, mysterious to her husband, though presumably her native Portuguese, and otherwise remains silent, never asking him questions. Rather than speak in one instance, for example, she "hatte sich schweigend geöffnet wie eine Rose" (GW6 258). All three men—explorer, warrior, and scientist—engage in conquest of some sort and wield intellect as their weapon or tool. They hunt, fight, or explore to acquire treasures—minerals, land, or knowledge. The women, on the other hand, are self-sufficient, at least in part because of their closeness to nature. Even Tonka, the domestic servant and shop girl of the big city, manages to provide for herself without ambition; her refusal to seek advancement and willingness to accept circumstances as they arise annoy her male friend.

The three women are foreign, from the south or east, and hence presented as exotic. The Portugiesin's beauty, we learn, provides an asset to the Ketten lineage by optimizing Ketten's chances of having attractive sons. Homo's fascination with Grigia stems in great measure from her exotic cultural mix of language and values indigenous to her secluded mountain valley and imported from western Europe. And Tonka's combination of Czech and German language and culture partly accounts for her appeal to her male friend.

The portrayal of the women in these three Novellen provides the strongest evidence of a retreat from principles of realism. The female characters are far more schematic than realistic. As discussed above, they are portrayed as otherworldly beings rather than inhabitants of a realistic milieu. The Portugiesin is never named. Though we eventually learn Grigia's actual name, she is called by a nickname created by Homo, who takes the name "Grigia" from the cow tended by the woman, one example of many associations of women with animals made by the narrator in this text. To cite another association of magic, nature, and sexual contact with a woman, the narrator states of a meeting between Grigia and Homo, "Das war alles genau so einfach und gerade so verzaubert wie die Pferde, die Kühe und das tote Schwein" (GW6 244). Clearly dispensing with realistic objectivity, the narrator creates his own set of mythical images.

The closest physical description of the Portugiesin depicts her as a composite of external attributes; she appears as an inaccessible, self-contained, silhouettelike figure. The description of her, focalized through Ketten, recalls Johannes' wish that his vague feelings might externalize themselves as a "Kleid, an dessen Falten [er sich] halten könnte" (cf 24). When Ketten arrives on a rare visit to the castle, the narrator states:

> Da war, als er kam, ein weiches hellgraues Kleid mit dunkelgrauen Blumen, der schwarze Zopf war zur Nacht geflochten, und die schöne Nase sprang scharf an das glatte Gelb eines beleuchteten Buchs mit geheimnisvollen Zeichnungen. Es war wie Zauberei. Ruhig saß, in ihrem weichen Gewand, mit dem Rock, der in unzähligen Faltenbächen herabfloss, die Gestalt, nur aus sich heraussteigend und in sich fallend; wie ein Brunnenstrahl; und kann ein Brunnenstrahl erlöst werden, außer durch Zauberei oder ein Wunder, und aus seinem sich selbst tragenden schwankenden Dasein ganz heraustreten? (GW6 259)

Despite the wealth of detail in this passage, the Portugiesin herself remains an abstract *Gestalt*, a mysterious entity whose physical appearance is never described realistically.

In place of characterization of figures modeled on "real life," the three women are presented as embodiments of all that their male counterparts are not. Besides the opposition between male and female personality traits (to the extent that personalites are revealed at all), the female characters are associated with the supernatural and thus opposed in kind to the worldly practicality of the male figures. Ketten's view of his wife as "die zauberhafte Portugiesin" (GW6 256), the narrator's designation of her as "die mondnächtige Zauberin" (262), and her enigmatic assertion at the end of the work about the possible divine origin of the mysterious cat compound the supernatural imagery. Even Ketten's soldiers suspect the woman of alliance with the devil (258). Tonka is presented as "das einfache Mädchen" and is associated with a religious sphere by analogy to the Holy Virgin of the Christian myth. Finally, the sensuality of the female characters—Grigia's earthy sexuality and the Portugiesin's "Zärtlichkeit"—complete the schematic portrayal of the women as essentially different, remote, and yet fascinating beings.

Despite the contrast between male and female spheres and personality traits, a hidden bond ties the male character to his apparent opposite. Defined by her function as all that he perceives himself not to be, the Portugiesin is nonetheless seen by Ketten as part of himself when he is sick with fever. When Ketten experiences the dissolution of his being in a vision of death, the narrator states, "Der Herr von Ketten und dessen mondnächtige Zauberin waren *aus ihm herausgetreten*" (262, emphasis added), indicating his vision of his wife as an aspect of himself. And when Homo refuses to accompany his wife on her trip despite the fact that he has never been separated from her for even a day, it is because their child has made their love "divisible" in his eyes (234); by existing in relation to her child and not exclusively in correspondence with his psyche, his wife loses any claim of reality for him. The bonds and responsibilities that would define her identity as distinct from their relationship consign their love to an esoteric plane ungrounded in realistic experience or action. Having thus forfeited her role in the action of the story, Homo's distant wife remains merely a motivating ideal, a function of the psychic needs of the protagonist.

This function of secondary characters as "covers" ("Bekleidungsstücke") or projections of the protagonists' psyches also informs the *Vereinigungen,* but a difference in narrative stance (as well as gender) distingushes them from *Drei Frauen* and accounts in part for the shift from the mimetic quality of the earlier works to the mythical tendency of the later Novellen. The narrators of the *Vereinigungen* present the feeling of strangeness or otherness of the unknown men distinctly as a perception of the characters. They are not mythicized directly by the narrators. For example, the narrator of "Versuchung der stillen Veronika" states of Veronika, "nie so sehr wie damals *erschienen ihr* die Männer nur als ein Vorwand, bei dem selbst man sich nicht aufhalten soll, für etwas anderes, das sich in ihnen nur ungenau verkörpern konnte" (209, emphasis added). And of Claudine's perception of the man she meets in the train the narrator of "Vollendung der Liebe" states, "Aber *sie fühlte* mit Lust, daß er ganz ungewiß blieb, ein Beliebiger, nur eine dunkle Breite von Fremdheit" (169, emphasis added). In contrast, the male protagonists' perceptions of the women in *Drei Frauen* are not clearly attributed to the figures but presented directly by the narrator.

In projecting the perspective of the protagonist without marking it as such grammatically, through direct attribution or indirect discourse for example, the narrator imparts authority to the images of the women and manipulates the reader's perception of these characters, which are accepted on first reading as realistic. Whereas the narrators of *Vereinigungen* employ the mimetic technique of representing ideas as contents of a character's mind, even of a "begriffsstarker" character, the narrators of *Drei Frauen* veil their presence behind the "cloaks" of figures and setting. Appearing to hold to the conventions of realistic narration, they in fact create myth. Highly constructed and ephemerally bound to the conditions of objective reality, these narratives nonetheless conceal their constructedness, transcending the particulars of history and mimesis surreptitiously.

The dominance of mythic structuration over mimetic representation heightens the significance of the formal relations; forms assume meanings extending far beyond their realistic referents. As discussed above, Ketten's castle is associated with his being, but it is occupied by a foreign power—foreign, as we have seen, in an existential, as well as a national, sense. The castle where the Portugiesin resides becomes a territory, in a symbolic as well as realistic sense, that Ketten must recapture in order to maintain his position as lord. On his visits to the castle, Ketten expects to encounter resistance from the mysterious occupying force. Instead he meets with compliance: "es geschah nicht so;" and reacts with the thought, "ist Zärtlichkeit nicht noch unheimlicher?" (259). The Portugiesin, who resides in Ketten's home (*Heimat*), incites in Ketten a feeling of *Unheimlichkeit*, uncanniness, literally "un-home-likeness." The sensation caused by the Portugiesin is contrasted with that which is familiar to Ketten: "Traulich erschienen ihm dagegen Kriegslist, politische Lüge, Zorn und Töten" (259). Though he feels, "Das andere...ist fremd wie der Mond," the narrator reveals nonetheless, "Der Herr von Ketten liebte dieses andere heimlich" (259).

The coincidence of that which is *unheimlich* and yet secretly loved and therefore at some level familiar (a combination of both apparently opposite meanings of *heimlich*) provides insight into the function of the opposition in these texts between male protagonists and female lovers, familiar and foreign, self and other. Ketten's uneasy sense of *Unheimlichkeit* and yet fascination with "das andere" could serve as a textbook example of the uncanny as Freud defined it in his essay "Das Unheimliche." According to Freud, the uncanny is anxiety caused by something that is overtly alien but secretly familiar. It is produced by a narcissistic tendency, a vestige of a primitive animistic conception of the universe, that holds the world to be governed by forces that in actuality emanate from the psyche.[11]

Homo reveals such a narcissistic tendency vis-a-vis his physical surroundings when he first enters the secluded valley and senses, "daß sich unter dem Aussehen dieser Gegend, das so *fremd-vertraut* flackerte wie die Sterne in mancher Nacht, etwas sehnsüchtig Erwartetes verberge" (235, emphasis added). Ketten's sense of *Unheimlichkeit* with his foreign wife, who resides in his *Heimat* (already associated with his "wahres Wesen"), his secret (*heim-lich*) love for her as "das andere," and the attenuation in Homo's world of the boundary between inner and outer, familiar and strange, create fictional worlds that reflect the psyche of the protagonist, and belie the realism suggested by some aspects of the narration.

The schematic portrayal of the female characters and the failure of the narrators to set their perspectives apart from those of the protagonists create fictional worlds that revolve around the protagonists as planets around the sun, to adapt a phrase from Walter Sokel's discussion of a similar constellation in Kafka's fiction. "Grigia" and "Die Portugiesin" reveal a structure of self-reflection, a "closed circuit" like that discerned by Sokel in "Das Urteil."[12] A fictional world functioning solely as a projection of the mind of a character precludes mimesis of external reality and becomes instead a "structural correlative of narcissism,"[13] much like the figures in primitive myths.

The fused perspective of narrator and figure[14] actually masks a unitary perspective. The narrative hides a narcissistic merging of self and world, subjective and objective reality. Rather than representing the world of independent persons and objects, characters and setting become impenetrable surfaces reflecting the psyche of the protagonist. Though born of extreme subjectivity, and thus departing from the tradition of mimetic realism, the discourse fails to indicate its source, thereby also foregoing the clearly acknowledged, open subjectivity posited by Theodor Adorno as the hallmark of modern literature.[15]

Narcissism is suggested on the thematic, as well as the structural level of "Die Portugiesin." Ketten's illness is at least in part one of narcissistic alienation from his wife. When he gazes into her eyes, an act by which he might gain access to her, communicate with, and thereby know her, he can discern only his own image reflected on their surface: "Wenn er seiner Frau in die Augen sah, waren sie wie frisch geschliffen, sein eigenes Bild lag obenauf, und sie ließen seinen Blick nicht ein" (GW6 265).

The remedy suggested by the sentence, "Ihm war zu Mut, es müßte ein Wunder geschehn, weil sonst nichts geschah..." implies that a miracle might cure his condition, possibly by shattering his narcissistic shell. Ketten's prescience that a miracle is needed to effect a change precipitates the final events leading to his recovery. The arrival of his wife's friend from Portugal provides him with the impetus to assert himself, and the mysterious cat appears as a miraculous sign of deliverance (Erlösung) from his debilitating condition. Scaling the wall of his castle and revitalizing his bond to his wife, which occasions the departure of his rival, release him from imprisonment within himself and reestablish the possibility of relationship to an independent other.

The mythic quality of *Drei Frauen* is highlighted by intertextual allusions to such familiar myths as the quest for identity with its origins in the *Odyssey* and the literature of the Middle Ages and its revival in the Romantic period. Claudine and Homo each undertake a journey that issues in union with another person—though in Homo's case also to his death—and intensifies the relationship fundamental to the protagonist's sense of identity.

Ketten's illness and recovery resemble in structure and theme the medieval epic, especially Hartmann von Aue's *Iwein*: The protagonists suffer a threat to existence at a moment of apparent well-being, enter a period of incapacitation and struggle for survival, and recover a measure of stability in the end. Ketten and Iwein both follow patterns of setting out to do battle and returning to spouse and to court, and both "heroes" create conflict for themselves by failing to cultivate their marital bonds in favor of waging traditional obligatory war.

The identity sought by Ketten, however, depends on factors that invert the medieval pattern. Whereas Iwein must attain *êre*, the recognition accorded one who fulfills the expectations of society, Ketten's sense of identity proceeds from an inner realm. He cures his sickness and reintegrates his dissipating existence, establishing a tenuous stability, first by opening himself to the possibility of a miracle and then by interpreting and responding to the *Sendung*, the miraculous sign, in a semiconscious physical act of strength. By climbing the unclimbable cliff wall he attains integration by over-coming his own physical weakness, reentering the castle and reaffirming his alliance to the Portugiesin, who, as we have seen, represents not only a potentially unfaithful wife, but alienated aspects of his own nature as well.

Homo's journey presents a modern version of a mythic Romantic quest. Homo joins an expedition to reopen gold mines, a task reminiscent of Tieck's "Runenberg" or Hoffmann's "Bergwerke zu Falun." The expedition is led by a man bearing a form of E. T. A. Hoffmann's assumed name, "Amadeus," and the surname "Hoffingott," possibly a parodic reference to Hoffmann and Romantic religiosity. Homo's trip occurs outside of normal time ("Es gibt im Leben eine Zeit, wo es sich auffallend verlangsamt, als zögerte es weiterzugehn oder wollte seine Richtung ändern" [234]), its temporal progress is marked by diurnal-nocturnal rotation and seasonal succession rather than dates on a calendar. The setting is explicitly referred to as *Märchengebilde* (233) and *Märchenwald* (240). The motifs of *Sehnsucht*, the hidden "sehnsüchtig Erwartetes," the erotic-mystical experience, and the dissolution of bonds to life all recall Romantic motifs. Even Homo's sentimental delight at the erotic thought of his wife's "scharlach-farbene Blume" (240) existing for him alone combine and parody Romantic schemata, raising, with good reason, the suspicion of satire of Romantic mysticism.[16]

Finally, with "Tonka," Musil again draws on a familiar myth in presenting Tonka's story as a version of the biblical narrative of Christ's parthenogenesis and passion and as a myth of sacrifice, reminiscent of both the Christian story and ancient tragedy. Though the links to these schemata are intentionally clouded—Tonka remains only a "halbgeborener Mythos" (GW6 303)—structural parallels, *Gleichnisse*, and reflections of the narrator evoke similarity. Hence, despite naturalistic descriptive passages such as the detailed portrayal of life in a large city and the physical effects of Tonka's pregnancy, and despite the apparent turn to a mimetic plot, the mythical structure of *Drei Frauen* clearly overrides its character as mimetic representation.

Aristotle insisted that the myth, or plot, of narrative exhibit closure. It should concern "a single whole and complete action with a beginning, middle, and end." He distinguishes such a mythos from history, which presents "not a single action but a single period....with a purely accidental relationship of one event to the others" (Potts 51). The requirement of closure stems from a presumption of cosmic unity, a universal whole in which every particular phenomenon has a place that determines its meaning and value. The closure of a poetic work thus would enable it to reflect the completeness of the universe and allow myth to embody absolute truth, to transcend the particularity of history. Such an insistence on closure, associated with the privilege of myth over history, appears at odds with the modern rejection of metaphysical systems, with an empirical, inductive approach to knowledge, and with Musil's intent to create new possibilities by breaking through outworn structures. This apparent contradiction in Musil's Novellen between intent and form will soon be examined.

The *Vereinigungen* exhibit a lesser degree of closure, formal and conceptual, than *Drei Frauen*. Claudine's supposed "completion" of her love is more climax than resolution, and as such lacks the finality of a conclusion, and the confrontation of Veronika and Demeter at the end of "Versuchung der stillen Veronika" hardly admits of conclusiveness. Musil best expressed the lack of formal unity of these works when he wrote that, rather than being read as book, they should be viewed spread out under glass a few pages at a time (T1 347).

In contrast, the "myths" of *Drei Frauen* have definite endings. Homo follows a funnel-shaped course, proceeding from life with books, plans, wife, and son to the narrow valley and then to the constriction of the mine shaft. His spirit moves in the opposite direction, breaking first from routine existence, then from the need to live, and finally attaining the ultimate release of death. Whether the reader focuses on the physical or the spiritual progress, the sense of an ending is strong.

Ketten also progresses through a course—from the stability of victory in battle to physical and psychic instability to the triumphant, indeed miraculous, accomplishment of the impossible. Again, the valuation of his final triumph remains open—"Es war nichts bewiesen und nichts weggeschafft" (GW6 269)—but structural closure and the concomitant sense of finality for the reader prevail, despite uncertainty regarding its meaning.

The plot of "Tonka" pursues a path from love to conflict (suspicion of infidelity), downfall (failure of her lover to believe her) and death, which implies a closed structure like that of tragic myth. The allusions to familiar myths, medieval, Romantic, or Christian/tragic, underscore the sense of closure, and the structural principle is mirrored in the enclosed architectonic spaces and circles prevalent in the works.

Closure has long been regarded as a feature of the Novelle. Tied to its apodictic nature, the closed form has been the foundation of theorists' preference for the Novelle as the prose form best suited to positing a truth about life—to expressing knowledge, venturing a "guess" about the human condition, in symbolic form. Paul Ernst, taking a defensive stance against what he saw as the dissolution of the Novelle in the early twentieth century, addressed the issue of closure when he wrote: "Unzweifelhaft hat die moderne Auflösung der Novelle ihren letzten Grund in tiefliegenden Ursachen: die relativistische Richtung des modernen Geistes ist jeder Form feindlich, bei der es eben Anfang und Ende, eine Ursache und eine feste Folge geben muß" (WB 85).

The apparently closed structure demanded by the conventions of the genre and its traditional mythic function of expressing truth would seem to belie the modernity of Musil's Novellen. If they seek to indicate a general, fixed order, an absolute concept of truth, then they constitute an anachronism in the era in which they were written, a time of ascendancy of the short story—the open form of rupture, shock, or momentary aperçu—reflecting the rejection of overarching systems and the desire to shatter illusions.

The Novellen of *Drei Frauen*, however, despite their closed structures, offer an alternative to the pretensions to logic and completeness suggested by "beginning and end, a cause and a definite consequence." Though structurally rounded off, they do not claim to represent a universal truth. The compact form of the Novelle serves not to totalize, to reflect an absolute and original order, but rather to present an example of a process that would arouse readers and incite an analogous process—intellectual and emotional—in them.

Goethe had asserted a similar function of closure in his 1827 commentary on Arisotle's poetics. In this essay, he defines the purpose of aesthetic closure (*Abrundung*) as cathartic effect on the audience. A drama or novel should, according to Goethe, set the mind of the recipient in motion. It should not send impose on its audience a moral imperative, but stimulate development of one's own ethical sensibility. The spectator, who, "um nichts gebessert nach Hause geh[t],"[17] has not been overpowered by a specific moral precept or plot of action. The purpose of closure is, rather, more broadly didactic—to engender a sense of "wonder" and move the spectator/reader to act toward the good that she determines in her heightened sense of awareness.

A similar concept of aesthetic closure can be seen to underlie Musil's effort to connect ethical and aesthetic purpose in works of literature. In his theoretical writings Musil rejects the constraints of systems and codes; he refuses the claim to scientific or moral exhaustiveness, to any form of *Totalitätsgedanke*. He seeks, rather, to give artistic form to improbabilities and exceptions. And yet, under the heading "Wesen der Dichtung" in his diary,

Musil asserted the exemplary nature of literature: "exempla docent. Lehre in Beispielen" (T1 489). In seeking to create new possibilities and exceptions and yet counter the limitations of totalizing thought, Musil draws on the concept of *Gestalt* and, within that context only, of closure.

The *Gestalt*, the whole created by an act of forming relations, can be seen as the basis of the modern poetics of myth that takes shape in Musil's Novellen. The relations formed through narrative design attain significance as act, and this act, rather than its static content or "moral," is communicated, as it is executed, by the work. "Truth" is a function of the intensity of the process and the formal coherence of the product, not of conformity to an original order. The act of forming relations—engaging both intellect and emotions, rational and nonrational faculties—establishes meaning for improbable events, inner and outer, and expands their potential significance. In his focus on new constellations, new paradigms, Musil accommodates the traditional exemplary claim of the Novelle to a modern inclination to openness.

Musil accomplishes this "modernization" by drawing on the convention of the Novelle by which, as expressed by A. W. Schlegel, the Novelle can and should recount the extraordinary and unique, but not by dissecting the event to establish cause and effect but by setting it forth positively and demanding belief for it ("dieses nicht motivirend zergliedern, sondern es eben positiv hinstellen und Glauben dafür fodern"). As with myth, the effectiveness of the Novelle rests on the power of the image, the paradigm (or parable), to incite faith. The appeal of such a work, as of a "Lebenslehre in Beispielen," is not to reason, but to an intuitive (emotional and intellectual) acceptance on the part of the recipient.

The third work of *Drei Frauen*, "Tonka," problematizes the notion of faithful acceptance of myth. The narrative is complicated by the fact that the narrator presents himself as a reader, a somewhat uncertain interpreter of the events he relates as his own story. Because the narrator and the protagonist appear as variants of each other, the narrator struggling to recall and interpret earlier events and his earlier perceptions of them, the controlling subjectivity traditionally occupying the core of the Novelle and essential to the convention of mediation dissolves and the authoritative source capable of evoking a response of conviction disappears.

The effacing of the boundary between narrative subject and the objects it represents threatens the structural opposition that is the productive tension of the Novelle. The confusion of narrator and protagonist and the resulting focus on the act of narration, the moment of enunciation, as inextricably bound to the story, culminates in "Die Amsel." The problematic relation between narrative subject and reader, highlighted in these last two of Musil's Novellen, will be discussed in the following chapter.

NOTES

1. In L.J. Potts, *Aristotle on the Art of Fiction: An English Translation of Aristotle's 'Poetics'* (Cambridge: Cambridge University Press, 1968) 20.

2. Gregory Lucente, *The Narrative of Realism and Myth* (Baltimore: Johns Hopkins University Press, 1981).

3. F. Schlegel, WB 41 (cf. 15 above); Lukacs, WB 91.

4. Robert Musil, *Briefe 1901-1942*, hrsg. Adolf Frisé (Hamburg: Rowohlt, 1981) 24. Also in Roth, *Ethik und Ästhetik*, 125.

5. Jakobson, 38.

6. Dorrit Cohn, *Transparent Minds: Narrative Modes for Presenting Consciousness in Fiction* (Princeton: Princeton University Press, 1978) 93. For a lucid discussion of the conflict between material and means of representation in Musil see also Walter H. Sokel, "Robert Musils Kampf um die Mimesis: Zur Poetologie seiner Anfänge," *Musil-Forum* 10 (1984) 238.

7. See Dorrit Cohn, "Psyche and Space in Musil's 'Vollendung der Liebe,'" *Germanic Review* 49 (1974) 154-168.

8. From a letter to Karl Baedeker, 16 August 1935, quoted in Roth, 282.

9. From Robert Musil Nachlaß, Mappe IV/3, 372f (A47). In Roth, *Ethik und Ästhetik*, 468f.

10. On the dialectical relationship between open spaces and enclosure as images of the mind in "Vollendung der Liebe," see Cohn, "Psyche and Space...," 160-162.

11. Sigmund Freud, "Das Unheimliche," *Gesammelte Werke* 12 (Frankfurt: Fischer, 1952).

12. Walter H. Sokel, "Frozen Sea and River of Narration: The Poetics behind Kafka's 'Breakthrough,'" *New Literary History* 17.2 (1986) 352f.

13. Sokel, "Frozen Sea," 353.

14. Cohn, "Psyche and Space...," 157.

15. See Theodor Adorno, "Standort des Erzählers im zeitgenössischen Roman," *Noten zur Literatur* I (Frankfurt: Suhrkamp, 1974) 61-73.

16. See Michael W. Jennings, "Mystical Selfhood, Self-Delusion, Self-Dissolution: Ethical and Narrative Experimentation in Robert Musil's 'Grigia'," *Modern Austrian Literature* 17.1 (1984) 59. Jennings asserts that the authorial voice conveys the danger of Homo's combination of mysticism and aggression. He argues "that a seemingly insoluble ethical contradiction—obedience to the sanctions of a (mystical) religion brings about violence and death—is made to cohere by appeal to a religion that is radically personal and, if projected onto society as a whole, spurious and untenable" (75).

17. Johann Wolfgang von Goethe, "Nachlese zu Aristoteles' Poetik," *Werke,* Hamburger Ausgabe 12, 9. Aufl. (München: Beck, 1981) 345.

CHAPTER FOUR

Subjectivity in "Tonka" and "Die Amsel"

As we have seen, tension between a narrating subject and an objective event provides the structural force that shapes the Novelle. The narrator orders the events recounted and thereby mediates them to the recipients of the narrative. The narrator's "subjective Stimmung und Ansicht" (F. Schlegel) structures the presentation of the realistic events portrayed. Lukács, as we have seen, distinguishes the Novelle from longer prose forms on just this basis: "Das Subjekt der kleineren epischen Formen steht beherrschender und selbstherrlicher seinem Objekte gegenüber," and "...immer ist es seine Subjektivität, die aus der maßlosen Unendlichkeit des Weltgeschehens ein Stück herausreißt, ihm ein selbständiges Leben verleiht und das Ganze...nur als Spiegelung einer an sich seienden Wirklichkeit in die Welt des Werks hineinscheinen läßt."[1] Even John Ellis, who denies prescriptive and even descriptive force to the term "Novelle," devotes his genre study *Narration in the German Novelle* to an examination of the relation of narrator to narrative.

Though Schlegel and Lukács agree that the subject should veil his presence in his discourse, thereby increasing the illusion of objectivity, the mythic mode that dominates *Drei Frauen* obscures the presence and identity of the narrator in such a way that the distinction between subject and object of representation breaks down. The uncertainty of the relation between narrator and protagonist, as well as the ostensibly mimetic narrative surface that conceals the subjective source of the fictional world, collapses the structure of mediation central to the Novelle. Narration becomes detached from an identifiable personal narrator and the reader can no longer locate the source of narrative authority. Wolfgang Kayser has argued that the dissolution of the personal narrator undermines epic narrative in the novel.[2] His argument applies all the more to the Novelle, since the absence of the personal mediator, the source of subjective control central to the genre, removes one of its critical structural members. If the Novelle is to achieve mediation, then knowledge of the identity and locus of the mediator would seem a condition for understanding and accepting the meaning he conveys.

The deliberate framing of many Novellen confirms the importance in the genre of locating and establishing the authority of the narrator(s). The problem of the relation between subject and object, the fused, or rather "con-fused," identity of narrator and protagonist observed in "Grigia" and "Die Portugiesin" intensifies in "Tonka" and "Die Amsel." In "Tonka" the use of the third-person pronoun creates uncertainty as the distance between narrator and hero is repeatedly modified and thus undermined by techniques typical of first-person narrative. In "Die Amsel," narrator(s) and characters are bound even more inextricably to one another, causing uncertainty about narrative control. Unable to locate the source of the narrative, the reader of "Die Amsel" either flounders, supporting Kayser's claim of the dissolution of the epic form, or seeks the narrative subject, the mediating instance, elsewhere than with a personal narrator.

Whereas the narrator's identity is obscured on the one hand, the issue of identity is raised as crucial on the other by an insistent existential component in the thematic structure of the Novellen. The quests for identity central to the first two works of *Drei Frauen* have been noted already; "Tonka" and "Die Amsel," too, portray narrators and protagonists facing the challenge of self-definition. They struggle against restrictive notions of self and yet attempt to assert and shape existence, to establish identity in a broad sense.

As the contours of the personal narrator, the subjective pole of the Novelle, dissipate in Musil's narratives, the burden placed on the reader increases. As discussed earlier, Musil held the task of the writer to be mediation of knowledge by mediating experience (GW8 1224). His attempt to engage the reader, to render the reading process more complex, can be seen in his striking analogies, which complicate, rather than ease, the reader's task, and in an overall indeterminacy that requires increased interpretive effort. With Wolfgang Iser one could characterize his goal as creation of more and wider gaps to be filled,[3] with Roland Barthes of an increasingly writerly, as opposed to readerly response.[4] A shift also occurs in the notion of "subject" that is forecast by the protagonists' assuming a receptive role as they begin to "read" events, objects, and people around them as signs and to interpret and respond to them.

While the narrative compels the reader to assume a more creative role, the narrators simultaneously relinquish control of the mediation process and take upon themselves the task of reading and interpretation. The narrators of "Tonka" and "Die Amsel," for example, seek to interpret their own discourse. They narrate in order to understand and to define themselves in an open-ended process of which they are both subject and object. They engage in mediation but do not control it. Positing an image through their discourse, they plot existence in order to establish identity, and yet the ground they stake out is not fixed, but remains as dynamic and changeable as the matter of which it is formed—language.

From the constellation of narrator, narration, and reader that takes shape in these works, a concept of subjectivity emerges that redefines the Novelle and yet carries out its traditional task of mediation. The subject-object tension based on the nineteenth-century concern for the position of the individual relative to his natural and social environment is replaced in Musil's Novellen by a concept of "subject" not centered around a given psychologically motivated individual, but existing in and through discourse—a linguistic construct rather than a personal figure. This concept of subjectivity rests on relation rather than essence, and the relations are established through language. Process and function are emphasized over stability and essence, producing a subject more open to change, redefinition, and possibility than the "Mensch mit dem festen Punkte a" (GW8 1026), Musil's prototype of the constrained and stagnant bourgeois individual.

This notion of subjectivity emerges most clearly in "Tonka" and "Die Amsel." The issue of subjectivity becomes central with the shift that occurs in the tension between subjectivity and objectivity in "Grigia" and "Die Portugiesin," when predominantly naturalistic (in Musil's sense of the term) narrative gives way to mythic structuration. In these texts, as we have seen, subjectivity dominates and yet hides itself in fiction, projecting a mythical image veiling its source. In "Tonka" and "Die Amsel" the subjective and authoritative function of the narrator merges with the traditional task of the reader—reading, interpretation, and response to the narration of the event being mediated.

In several passages in his journals and essays, Musil states his intent to engender a new reader for and through

his works. He writes, "Th. M. [Thomas Mann] und ähn-
liche schreiben für die Menschen, die da sind; ich schreibe
für Menschen, die nicht da sind" (TB1 880). The task of the
writer, he asserts, is to discover "lockende Vorbilder, wie
man Mensch sein kann, den inneren Menschen erfinden"
(GW8 1029). If readers respond in accordance with this
design, then new possibilities for existence—and, as we
will see, for new subjectivity—arise through the reading
process. The antagonism of readers toward Musil's first
Novellen, *Vereinigungen*, resulting at least in part from
the increased demands placed on them by these texts,
reveals the disparity between the potential ideal reader
envisioned by Musil (or, for that matter, any ideal image
of the reader) and actual readers.

In discussing the purpose of literature with regard to
the reader, Musil indicated concern with aesthetic effect.
He viewed effect, however, not as an end in itself, but as a
means of conveying knowledge, of mediating *Erkenntnis* by
mediating *Erlebnis*. According to this view, literature is
meant to communicate, not by transferring information or
reflecting a state of affairs, but by stimulating the reader
to respond—to read signs and react to them. In a passage in
the tenth notebook of his diary, Musil anticipates Iser's
theory of reader response by articulating, from the writer's
perspective, how readers' participation is coerced: "Ein
Weg, der in das Wesen der Dichtung führt, ist die
Beachtung der Tatsache, daß Andeutung stärker wirkt als
Ausführung" (T1 470). Incomplete objects, a crude doll for a
child or a smooth stone for a dog, for example, engage the
imagination, Musil wrote. The observer completes the
object, supplies the details—or, in Iser's terms, fills in the
gaps—supplementing the text in the act of reception.[5]

In his attempt to engage the reader, to elicit response
rather than present a literary *fait accompli* to a passive
receiver, Musil assumes a position within the Platonic
tradition of knowledge and foregoes a purely empirical

epistemological stance. According to the intellectual tradition associated with Leibniz and the hermeneutical epistemology of Schleiermacher and Dilthey, knowledge entails participation, engagement with an object or idea. Understanding must be incited and evoked, not merely imprinted upon the mind of a passive observer as on a *tabula rasa*. In this view, the conveyance and acquisition of knowledge resembles religious experience as discussed, for example in a book by Rudolf Otto, a theologian and contemporary of Musil. In *Das Heilige* (1917) Otto asserts the importance of inspiring, inciting the listener, engaging emotional and even physical, as well as rational faculties to impart religious precepts.[6] The goal of such discourse for the recipient is a state in which activity and receptivity combine. "Tonka" and "Die Amsel" engage the complex dialectical interplay between activity and receptivity in knowing and narrating.

In the essay "Der deutsche Mensch als Symptom" Musil assigns a crucial role in the epistemological process to the emotional state of an observer of inanimate objects as of human beings. The viewer's attitude, he argues, beyond simply affecting the observer, actually changes the object itself:

> Daß ein Mensch sich vollkommen verändert, je nachdem man ihn mit Sympathie oder ohne solche betrachtet, ist bekannt, und unsre Wissenschaft kann man geradezu als sympathielose Betrachtung beschreiben.... Man wird da allerdings fragen, ob sich denn wirklich auch leblose Dinge verändern, je nachdem man sie mit oder ohne Liebe betrachtet, und ich möchte diese Frage bejahen. (GW8 1392)

Reception thus involves a degree of activity in Musil's view.

"Tonka" and "Die Amsel" illustrate the converse idea—that narrating, a creative act, entails receptivity as well. The interplay of active and receptive attitudes toward experience appears in these Novellen as a precarious, but necessary, balance for the narrators and protagonists. The knowledge acquired through this kind of active reception allows a fuller, and thus more accurate, perception than that attained through the "sympathielose Betrachtung" of empirical science.

The protagonists of Musil's Novellen are transformed into readers of sorts as they proceed on a course toward self-definition and -assertion. These characters suffer from a tension between the desire for *Selbstauflösung*, dissolution of the self, and *Selbstsucht*, an intensified, nearly pathological, *Selbstsuche*, a search for the self. They struggle with the need for self-assertion and stability (coherence, continuity, identity) and the equally strong urge for freedom, flexibility, and change. The drive toward dissolution converges with the desire for intense experience, for transcendence of limits, which, however, entails loss of individual identity. The thematic concern with identity and responsibility appears to be subverted by a narrative technique that bars identification of the narrator and distinction from the protagonist. As Susan Erickson writes, "Musil's questioning of historical 'texts' simultaneously deconstructed and demanded ... a ['centered'] self."[7]

The tension between the drive toward dissolution and a heightened sense of self emerges in the early Novelle "Vollendung der Liebe" in Claudine's vacillating evaluation of feelings of confinement and expansion. Enclosure is adjudged intense self-awareness and self-definition at one moment and restriction of freedom at the next. In "Versuchung der stillen Veronika" the protagonist alternately loses a sense of individuality, of distinction from the objects surrounding her, and then gains, in contrast, a "Gefühl von sich," a heightened awareness of self.[8]

The protagonists of "Grigia" and "Die Portugiesin" seek a locus of stability, an edifice or plane within, but distinguishable from, the world around them. At the same time they resist confinement within this space. Homo senses a conflict between *Selbstauflösung* and *Selbstsucht* as he deliberates whether to travel with his wife and son or remain behind with his books, plans, and his life, and he (or the narrator?) cannot discern which of these feelings actually occupy him: "[Homo] empfand seinen Widerstand als eine große Selbstsucht, es war aber vielleicht eher eine Selbstauflösung..." (GW6 234). In "Die Portugiesin" Ketten suffers mental and physical threat of dissolution, but the ebbing of his strength finally leads to assertion of identity.

"Tonka" and "Die Amsel" not only address identity but also raise the ethical question of the legitimacy of the self and its actions. The issue of identity and the implications of losing it are raised in the second paragraph of "Tonka" by the narrator's statement, "Es ist nicht zufällig, daß es in seinem Militärjahr war, denn niemals ist man so entblößt von sich und eigenen Werken wie in dieser Zeit des Lebens, wo eine fremde Gewalt alles von den Knochen reißt" (GW6 270). The penultimate paragraph of the narrative considers the effect of Tonka's life on the protagonist in explicitly ethical terms: "Und vieles fiel ihm seither ein, das ihn besser machte als andere, weil auf seinem glänzenden Leben ein kleiner warmer Schatten lag. Das half Tonka nichts mehr. Aber ihm half es" (GW6 306). The narrator thereby emphasizes the ethical bearing of Tonka's story on her friend's life. While ostensibly telling the story of Tonka, the narrative has been designed, it now appears in retrospect, to legitimate the protagonist, to establish his identity and redeem him by setting him in relation to her.

The pattern of concern with the self culminates in the seemingly urgent attempt of A2 to tell and justify his life's story in "Die Amsel." A2 narrates his life, creating a plot that strongly resembles a confession; he, too, concludes with a proclamation that he is "ein guter Mensch," though he cannot describe what a good person is (GW7 562). In his narrative A2 seizes on isolated moments in his life and tries to integrate them into an image in which he can find meaning and value. In his search A2 reads events and perceptions as signals of dissolution of a restrictive fixed identity (*Selbstauflösung*) and at the same time of the intense occupation with defining a new one (*Selbstsucht*).

The question of identity frames "Die Amsel," but it is problematized immediately. The frame narrator introduces the character, "den [er] erwähnen muß, um drei kleine Geschichten zu erzählen, bei denen es darauf ankommt, wer sie erzählt" (GW7 548); but after claiming that it matters who tells the stories, he explains neither his acquaintance with the new narrator, A2, nor why it is he who should narrate. Further, he undermines the very notion of identity by describing A2's self as the "verschiedene Herren...die er der Reihe nach mit Ich anspricht," and "dieses, kleine, alberne, ichige Scheusal" (GW7 548). A2 also expresses annoyance at the idea of a stable identity in resenting his mother's clinging to a fixed image of him, and yet he tells the story of three significant experiences from his life in order to ascertain its meaning. He finally withdraws into the room where he spent his childhood and becomes keenly interested in the books he once read there, apparently "finding himself" in a regressive quest that parodies the Romantic notion of return of the hero in, for example, Novalis' *Heinrich von Ofterdingen*. A2 also keeps a caged blackbird, which he associates with his mother, indicating narcissistic inability to separate from her and establish a mature, independent identity.

Two passages in the *Vereinigungen* suggest a radical interdependence between identity and language, which reaches an apex in the last two Novellen. In "Vollendung der Liebe" Claudine compares the tension between continuity and dissolution of the self with discourse:

> Sie dachte, man gräbt eine Linie ein, irgendeine bloß zusammenhängende Linie, um sich an sich selbst zwischen dem stumm davonragenden Dastehn der Dinge zu halten; das ist unser Leben; etwas wie wenn man ohne Aufhören spricht und sich vortäuscht, daß jedes Wort zum vorherigen gehört und das nächste fordert, weil man fürchtet, im Augenblick des abreißenden Schweigens irgendwie unvorstellbar zu taumeln und von der Stille aufgelöst zu werden; aber es ist nur Angst, nur Schwäche vor der schrecklich auseinanderklaffenden Zufälligkeit alles dessen, was man tut...." (GW6 185)

The narrator of "Versuchung der stillen Veronika" similarly compares language and self: "doch fühlte sie nichts als sich und wo sie ging, war sie und war nicht, wie unausgesprochene Worte manchmal in einem Schweigen" (GW6 218). Claudine and Veronika both question the possibility of an integral, fixed self as of a continuous, integrated and integrating narrative line. While undermining the ontological status of both self and narrative, however, Claudine is also frightened by the consequences of its absence: Silence causes dissipation and condemns words and actions to random contingency. Though she prefers silence and nothingness ("ein Stillwerden, ein Nichts" [185]) to inauthentic speech, she expresses a desire to create in language an authentic and yet flexible self which might be asserted amid "dem stumm davonragenden Dastehn der Dinge."

In the tenth notebook of his journal Musil defines consciousness as standing in a relationship or context ("in einem Zusammenhang stehen" [TB 451]). He continues, "Verschieden im Menschenleben sind weder die Fakta noch die inneren Zustände, sondern ihre raumzeitliche Anordnung./ Individuum ist ein Ablauf, eine Variation. Fertig mit seinem Tod" (TBI 452). Relation, not substance, defines consciousness, and relations are structured like the syntax of language. Like a word in a sentence, the individual derives identity and meaning from an ordering of relations in time and space. Language creates the "raumzeitliche Anordnung" in narrative discourse that is the individual, the "self," and that self is an ongoing process, always subject to variation.

The narrative acts of "Tonka" and "Die Amsel" complicate the process of creating subjectivity through language and add a new dimension to the enterprise of mediation carried out and thematized by the Novelle in that they graft an element of receptivity to that process. To establish themselves as "selves," the narrators of "Tonka" and "Die Amsel" take on the role of reader as well as of narrative subject. Mediating from a position of incomplete control, they engage in a dynamic, open-ended process that reflects neither a given origin nor a final meaning. Rather than presenting a particular image of a general truth, Musil's Novellen sketch partially delineated, implied possibilities, which cohere as *Gestalt* independent of an authoritative personal subject. And yet despite the loss of authoritative control, the act of positing an image, tenuous as it may be, is crucial to the existence of the narrator. The process of forming relations—creating an authentic and coherent, however fleeting, *Gestalt*—forestalls dissolution of the self. Rather, by delineating a structure (an *Anordnung*) in discourse, it establishes and situates the "self" in a set of relations (*Zusammenhang*). The narrator has no privileged notion of the meaning of his *Gestalt* previous to its formation but must read it to recognize and make sense of his own subjectivity.

The need for the narrative subject to assume a second function of receptive audience parallels the course toward heightened receptivity of the protagonists who most often determine the narrative perspective of the narrators in *Drei Frauen*. Homo, Ketten, and Tonka's friend exist initially as men of action—scientists, explorers, planners, warriors—who assume a progressively more receptive attitude toward people and objects in their fictional surroundings. Though Homo initially declines to accompany his family because he fears separation from himself (GW6 234), he does leave his previous occupations and develops an obsessive fascination with a foreign valley that promises to hold something for which he has yearned and waited, rather than actively pursuing (235). In an attempt to gain access to its hidden meanings, he reads objects and events as signs. Figural language—the comparisons with "wie" and conjectures with "als" and the subjunctive—express his interpretive transformations of his surroundings, making of him both a reader and a poet who creates metaphors: The flowers in the field look to him like the fairy-tale *Sterntaler* (236), the village women become "stillgewordene Tiere" (237) under his glance, and a farmer with a sickle takes on the identity of "der leibhafte Tod" (237) in Homo's eyes (and the narrator's language). Homo responds emotionally when he recognizes and reads his son's handwriting on a letter and finds that it sheds an entirely new light on his situation (240). The "Tiersprache" of his fellow explorers are perceived as "Zeichen" (243), which invite deciphering, and horses in a field are arranged in a pattern following "einem geheim verabredeten ästhetischen Gesetz" (242), which, too, demands interpretation or decoding (242). His inclination to read and interpret objects, people, and events as signs culminates in his experience of "Fernliebe," which he perceives as centered on the erotic metaphor, "the scarlet flower," and which he raises to the height of religious significance:

> Zwischen den Geheimnissen dieser Natur war das Zusammengehören eines davon. Es gab eine scharlachfarbene Blume, es gab diese in keines anderen Mannes Welt, nur in seiner, so hatte es Gott geordnet, ganz als ein Wunder. Es gab eine Stelle am Leib, die wurde versteckt und niemand durfte sie sehn, wenn er nicht sterben sollte, nur einer. Das kam ihm in diesem Augenblick so wundervoll unsinnig und unpraktisch vor, wie es nur eine tiefe Religion sein kann. (240)

Although Homo actively transforms his surroundings into a fairy-tale world, on the one hand, he casts aside the agency and responsibility usually associated with the subjective role, on the other, in refusing to write to his wife. (The narrator, however, who has shared Homo's vantage point and interpretive inclination, maintains his stance as subjective agent of narration throughout the Novelle, even after Homo has died.)

In "Die Portugiesin" Ketten moves from the role of aggressor—a "wolf" circling his prey—to that of listless observer who, forced by circumstances, learns to read events as signs. Receptivity to signs and response to them actually bring on his recovery. Although the climb up the cliff wall into the castle requires active exertion, Ketten garners the strength he needs by *re*-acting: First, the foreign "Zeichen" by which his wife communicates with her childhood friend impel him to challenge the developing intimacy between them. Then the impenetrability of his wife's gaze provokes him to anticipate a resolution and triggers his recovery. When he sees his wife's face reflecting his own like a mirror, he concludes, "[man] *soll horchen*, was kommen wird" (GW6 265, emphasis added), and a resolution quickly follows. As soon as he becomes receptive to the possibility of a miracle, the small cat arrives at the gate (265) and its "martyrdom" follows. Ketten's receptive state, as opposed to the activity by which he had formerly sought to control the world, precipitates the mystery. Ketten and the other adults attribute great significance to the cat's death, expecting meaning to emerge from it, whereas the children find it quite normal. Though there is no verbal exchange between Ketten and the Portugiesin, the narrator voices their question of how to interpret and respond to the mysterious event, "Das Zeichen war da gewesen, aber wie war es zu deuten und was sollte geschehn?" (268).

The story comes to a conclusion when Ketten does interpret (*deutet*) and then acts upon the impulse of the sign, the death of the cat. His half-conscious, partially intuitive interpretation and reaction (an *Urentscheidung*, as used by A2 in "Die Amsel") finally answer the question of "was sollte geschehn."

The question from "Die Portugiesin," "Das Zeichen war dagewesen, aber wie war es zu deuten und was sollte geschehn?" could be said to occupy the narrators and protagonists (whose identities become even less distinct) of Musil's last two Novellen. "Tonka" and "Die Amsel" reveal the significance of receptivity and response for the narrative subject, whose authority wanes as he becomes concerned with reception. His receptive role is marked by openness, and narrative form reflects this state. Two questions confront the narrators/protagonists—the hermeneutic question of how to interpret events and people in the fictional worlds, and the ethical one of how to respond to them. Both questions have an existential dimension in that they require an active choice that defines "self" or "subject."

The narrator of "Tonka" tells the story of the association of a young man, presumably himself at an earlier stage of consciousness, with Tonka; in retrospect he constructs a plot, attempting to create a myth that would bear meaning and truth for him. His narration of Tonka's story serves as a means of self-definition for its narrator. The authority of his stance as narrative subject and mediator, however, and his control over and access to the events he recounts are called into question.

The (con-)fused relationship between narrator and protagonist discussed in the previous chapter in connection with "Grigia" and "Die Portugiesin" becomes more critical in "Tonka." The authority of the narrator is undermined by lack of definition of his relation to the protagonist and to the events he recounts. This uncertainty emerges in the opening paragraphs, subverting the convention of the frame that served to establish narrative authority in many traditional Novellen, Storm's *Der Schimmelreiter* providing the most illustrative example. Preceding the more conventionally realistic exposition of Tonka's past, the Novelle opens with a string of fragmentary recollections and reflections suggesting first-person narration. The narrator appears to question himself, his memory, and his judgment, when he asks, "Ist es Kleinlichkeit, wenn solche Einzelheiten sich an einen Menschen heften? Wie Kletten!?" (GW6 270). Not until the second paragraph is the protagonist distinguished grammatically from the narrator; the pronoun "er" forces the reader to reconstruct his initial vision of the subject-object (*ich/er*) constellation.

In the third paragraph the narrator calls attention to the distinction between past events and the fiction being constructed to recount—and account for—them: "Aber war es überhaupt so gewesen? Nein, das hatte er sich erst später zurechtgelegt. Das war schon das Märchen; er konnte es nicht mehr unterscheiden" (270). The narrator reminds the reader again of the fictionality of his narrative two pages later: "....aber das war doch nicht damals gewesen, denn das, was eben wie Erinnerung erscheinen wollte, war schon wieder das später gewachsene Dornengerank in seinem Kopf" (272). Both these "apologia" are followed by the phrase, "In Wahrheit...," marking in the first instance an end to the opening frame and signaling in both cases a shift from the questioning discourse to the telling of the story and asking that this be taken as "truth."

Narrator, protagonist, and reader all have difficulty determining the validity of their perceptions and interpretations of the events of the story. The narrator seems to view them from a greater distance than the protagonist, and yet as the narration proceeds, the reader loses sight of the controlling subjectivity, the source of the thoughts, perceptions, and recollections voiced at any given moment. The distance between narrator and protagonist constantly fluctuates, but it gradually diminishes as the narrative progresses, to the point where the "Dornengerank," and the "Märchen," of which the narrator speaks, seem actually to refer self-reflexively to the narrative itself.

Although the narrator speaks of Tonka's friend in the third person, the fusion of his point of view with the protagonist's obscures the relation of the narrator's discourse to the story he tells and suggests the identity of narrator and protagonist at the end. Whereas the narrators of the earlier Novellen, "Grigia" and "Die Portugiesin," ultimately distinguish themselves from the characters, the apparent but unacknowledged identity of narrator and protagonist at the end of "Tonka" raises suspicion about the motivation for the narration.

In a study of narrative technique in Musil's Novellen, Brigitte Röttger demonstrates that narrative technique renders "Tonka" a combination of first-and third-person narrative.[9] "Tonka" also exhibits characteristics posited by F. Stanzel as typical of a confessional (first-person) form[10] in that its structure is defined by tension between an experiencing and a reflecting "I." Moreover, it features the element of *Umkehr*, an inner conversion or change of heart often found in autobiography. Despite the third-person pronoun, Stanzel's definition of autobiography captures the narrative situation of "Tonka": "Im Ich-Roman versucht sich ein Mensch selbst zu begreifen, sich zu definieren, von seiner Umwelt abzugrenzen" (36).

Peter Henninger carries this argument further, claiming that the combination of third-person pronoun and preterite tense typical of third-person narration with a conversational form typical of discourse in the first person produces a "radical equivocation" that subverts the norms of representational (epic) narration. Henninger holds the meshing of subject and object to be an error, a "Webfehler im Text", revealing a condition of split subjectivity in its author.[11]

Even without equating the subject of the narrative with the psyche of its author, the concept of subjectivity and its function in the work can be called into question when the narrative agency is removed from an identifiable narrator. "Tonka" does, as Henninger claims, undermine the notion of a stable subject, not of its author, however, but of its narrator. The model of the subject as a unified, psychological entity is replaced by a functional or relational model.

The narrator of "Tonka" seeks neither to represent nor to interpret the title figure but to define himself in relation to her. Of a year in which the protagonist is "entblößt von sich," the narrator constructs a myth, a *Märchen*, as he says, designed to assign meaning to, and further, to redeem, his own action. The act of narration is at once an act of interpretation and of attempted effect—salvation.

The myth coheres, however, only as the events are viewed and recounted in retrospect. The narration serves as an act of mediation not by presenting authorial knowledge of events and an understanding of their significance but by questioning and only provisionally interpreting them. The narrator "reads" the image he has created as a myth of redemption, of deliverance from guilt, as a Christian would read the story of Christ's life. He structures and colors the events after the "fact" in order to attribute mythical significance and redemptive power to Tonka. At the time of narration—in retrospect, that is—he claims, "Tonka war in die Nähe tiefer Märchen gerückt. Das war die Welt des Gesalbten, der Jungfrau und Pontius Pilatus..." (289). Tonka dies without bearing her child, however, and with no sign of resurrection; she falls far short of mythic status in any but the narrator's eyes. At the conclusion of his narrative, he himself admits that the myth has remained "halbgeboren."

Although the narrator attributes the failure of the myth to insufficient power on Tonka's part ("Vielleicht war Tonka's Kraft zu gering" [GW6 303]), his own failed narrative authority better explains the aborted myth. Its insufficient force results from his inadequate authority, because as subject of the narrative, he cannot guarantee its truth.

Particularly characteristic of this Novelle and a source of its intrigue and accomplishment, the failure of the narrator/protagonist of "Tonka" is born of a receptive dysfunction as well. Bound to rationality, which he cannot cast aside, he cannot summon the faith that would complete the myth and raise it to the status of transcendent truth. His failed authority contributes to his receptive dilemma; he can never be assured of the truth of the myth because he is aware of the limitations of its author and the tentativeness of his discourse. Unable to rely on the text of his narration nor to accept it on faith, he feels his access to "truth" reduced to moments of involuntary insight, fleeting revelations which cast a "kleine[n] warme[n] Schatten" but provide no ultimate certainty.

Early in the narrative, the narrator implies that the need for clear distinctions and frustration with ambiguity that plague the protagonist—both related to his inability to accept Tonka's innocence on faith—are conditions to which men are more susceptible than women. The distress caused by uncertainty accounts at least in part for the differences between Tonka and her friend and her inaccessibility to him. When he first encounters Tonka's female relatives and hears of the sexual conduct of Tonka's cousin Julie, he is surprised by the women's interaction with her: "Er wunderte sich darüber, daß man sich mit Kusine Julie an einen Tisch setzen und ihr eine Tasse Kaffee zuschieben konnte, denn sie war doch eine Schande" (270). Just as he later becomes obsessed with the question of Tonka's possible infidelity and his response to it, he reacts with the thought, "Ein Mann hätte ja vielleicht Lärm geschlagen, denn ein Mann liest die Zeitung oder gehört einem Verein mit bestimmten Zielen an und hat immer die Brust voll mit großen Worten..." (270). For Tonka's aunt, on the other hand, "...wenn man auch mißbilligte, fehlte die Kluft; man konnte hinüber" (271). The protagonist also finds it peculiar that Tonka and her grandmother come into regular contact with women from a local jail.

Were he able to accept ambiguity as unproblematic, as do the women in this society, the conflict between faith and knowledge would not prevent him from responding to Tonka nor entail such a rupture in his life; he finds, however, that for him the rift *is* too broad to span. He pursues facts and insists on interpreting them with the certitude of science, that is, of statistical probability, and to respond accordingly. His desire for scientific closure, for a probable explanation for Tonka's condition other than disloyalty, mirrors the narrator's desire to impose mythic closure on "Tonka."

The narrator's drive to interpret and to attain closure takes on force as the narrative progresses. At the beginning of his friendship with Tonka, he is unable to hide his frustration at her lack of ambition and inability to explain her feelings. In annoyance bordering on anger, he tries to force her to articulate her desires and thoughts. Then, in despair, he attempts to accommodate her pregnancy and illness to his interpretive framework, grounded in and limited by reason. He interprets smiles—hers (299), his mother's (273), the doctors' (292) and others' (303)—as signs, reading them as indications of incredulity, condescension and scorn, as confirmation of Tonka's guilt and his own naiveté. But smiles, he discovers, are over-determined signs permitting of no conclusive interpretation. Finally, maintaining a vigil over every potential indicator of Tonka's fidelity or infidelity, he attaches significance to expressions, movements, and gestures and the mark on her calendar.

The narrator explicitly acknowledges the difference between the original occurrences and interpretations of them when he says: "Das waren gewiß lauter kleine Erlebnisse, aber das Merkwürdige ist: sie waren in Tonkas Leben zweimal da, ganz die gleichen. Sie waren eigentlich immer da. Und das Merkwürdige ist, sie bedeuteten später das Gegenteil von dem, was sie anfangs bedeuteten" (GW6 278). Uncertainty remains; though the time indicator "später" reveals the distance between experiencing and reflecting subject, it leaves the question of their relation unresolved. *Später* is most probably the "now" of the narration, which would identify narrator and protagonist as the same person at different points in time, but this relation is never confirmed.

As Tonka's pregnancy proceeds (and the moment of birth/death approaches), the protagonist's occupation with interpretation reaches the point of obsession as he succumbs to superstition. Imputing significance to trivia—his ring, his beard and his potential winnings in the horse lottery (294)—he treats these normally insignificant objects and events as signs of good or ill fortune: "Ja selbst wenn sie nur fünf Mark gewonnen hätten, so wäre das ein Zeichen gewesen, daß der Versuch, wieder Anschluß an das Leben zu gewinnen, in unbekannten Gegenden wohlgelitten war" (294).

His compulsion to interpret memories of events and gestures and his despair at achieving certainty reaches its apex in the following passage. Despite its length, it repays consideration as evidence of the intense conflict between the unrelenting urge to interpret and the persistent doubt that the opposite interpretation holds true:

> Diese Gewißheiten über Tonkas Untreue hatten etwas von Träumen. Tonka ertrug sie mit ihrer rührenden, wortlos zärtlichen Demut: aber was konnte diese nicht alles bedeuten!? Und wenn man dann alle Erinnerungen durchging, wie waren alle zweideutig! Die einfache Art zum Beispiel, wie sie ihm zugelaufen war, konnte Gleichgültigkeit sein oder Sicherheit des Herzens. Wie sie ihm diente, war Trägheit oder Seligkeit. War sie anhänglich wie ein Hund, so mochte sie auch jedem Herrn folgen wie ein Hund! Das hatte er doch gleich in jener ersten Nacht empfunden, und war es auch ihre erste Nacht? Er hatte nur auf die seelischen Zeichen geachtet und keinesfalls waren die körperlichen sehr merklich gewesen. Jetzt war es zu spät. Ihr Schweigen war jetzt über alles gebreitet und vermochte Unschuld oder Verstocktheit zu sein, ebensogut List und Leid, Reue, Angst; aber auch Scham für ihn. Doch hätte es ihm nicht geholfen, wenn er auch alles noch einmal hätte erleben können. Mißtraue einem Menschen, und die deutlichsten Anzeichen der Treue werden geradezu

Zeichen der Untreue sein, traue ihm, und hand-
greifliche Beweise der Untreue werden zu Zeichen
einer verkannten, wie ein von den Erwachsenen
ausgesperrtes Kind weinenden Treue. Es war nichts
für sich zu deuten, eines hing von dem andern ab,
man mußte dem Ganzen trauen oder mißtrauen, es
lieben oder für Trug halten, und Tonka kennen hieß
in einer bestimmten Weise auf sie antworten müssen,
ihr entgegenrufen, wer sie sei. (296)

In pointing to the subjective attitude—trust and love or
mistrust—of the would-be knower as central to the truth to
which he aspires, this passage also establishes a clear
connection between the act of interpretation and the need
to answer to Tonka. The narrator acknowledges that he can
make such a choice to respond, accept responsibility or not.
He has the power to confirm Tonka's identity by responding with belief, to love "das Ganze," or consider himself
deceived and never know her.

Tonka takes on the significance of a *Sendung* for her
friend (298). He appropriates her existence as a source of
mysterious meanings: "es brauchte in ihm bloß Tonkas
Dasein anzuklingen, und ein Leben von Figuren begann, die
einander ablösten, ohne ihren Sinn zu verraten..." (299).
Finally he comes close to denying her existence, focusing
solely on its significance for him: "Dabei fiel ihm ein ...
das war gar nicht Tonka, mit der er gelebt hatte, sondern es
hatte ihn etwas gerufen" (306).

The narrator further reveals his function as reader
when he asserts his need to be convinced (297), a need of a
recipient and interpreter rather than authoritative subject
who would normally do the convincing. And as protagonist, he rejects the authorial role by destroying letters he
has written to his mother (296). Though he writes letters
to Tonka, "...Briefe, in denen er vieles sagte, was er sonst
verschwieg," he neglects to send them because "sie waren

waren ja nicht mit Sicherheit seine Meinung, sondern eben
ein Zustand, der sich nicht anders helfen kann als mit
Schreiben" (304). The function assigned to writing as
therapy underscores its transformation from a creative,
assertive act into one of reaction and response, a nearly
involuntary and almost desperate reflex that has slipped
beyond the writer's control.

The questions of response and responsibility ultimately
motivate the myth of "Tonka." The conclusion of the passage cited above shows that the despair of Tonka's friend
at the *Zweideutigkeit* of her behavior springs from concern
for his responsibility—his ability to respond to her
appropriately and the effect of success or failure:
"...Tonka kennen, hieß in einer bestimmten Weise auf sie
antworten müssen, ihr entgegenrufen wer sie sei; es hing
fast nur von ihm ab, was sie war" (296). He feels called
upon to answer to her and thereby determine for her and
others her identity. And yet in the end his narrative
reflects only his self-understanding; he tells her story in
his own interest, to the exclusion of hers.

Tonka's friend's feelings of guilt permeate his discourse
in many instances as he acknowledges responsibility
toward Tonka but doubts his fulfillment of it. Beginning
with his decision to bring her to his grandmother's house,
described as a "kleine List" and as "leichtsinnig" (274),
his sense of guilt persists while she works there, to the
point that he begs at one moment, "'Schimpfen Sie
weningstens auf uns!'" (274). When he promises to care for
her, the narrator states, "er....war über die Verantwortung
betreten, die er plötzlich auf sich geladen hatte" (281).
And though the doctors determine that Tonka must be
"geschont und gepflegt" (289) if she is to survive her
condition, his studies consume the couple's meager
resources, and his devotion to his academic career prevents
him from earning enough money to save Tonka from living
in a state of "Dürftigkeit, an der er die Schuld trug" (290).

In addition, as the friend is made aware by his mother, he controls Tonka's social status as well and can choose to make her either a whore or a wife. The narration of the story of Tonka's guilt thus ultimately reveals a preoccupation with the narrator's own.

The final line of "Tonka" provides evidence that concern with response actually motivates the narrative. The narrator concludes with an apologia of sorts, the speculation "daß das menschliche Leben zu schnell fließt, als daß man jede seiner Stimmen recht hören und *die Antwort auf sie finden könnte*" (306, emphasis mine). Asserting the need to hear and respond to "life's voices," he also declares the difficulty of the attempt.

The narrator/protagonist cannot evade guilt; his failing is that of the modern, rational scientist. In his approach to Tonka, as to all objects of knowledge, her friend uses her as an instrument, finally recognizing only her utility to him. Having condemned members of his family for slighting Tonka in order to promote their own interests at his grandmother's death, his insistence on principles of rationality causes him to carry on his family's abuse of her. By consigning Tonka to the category of mystical *Sendung*, he dehumanizes her. Further, "...[o]bgleich er längst an sie glaubte...," he refuses to declare his faith because, "Es hielt ihn heil und an der Erde fest, daß er das nicht tat" (304).

The most insidious means by which the narrator denies Tonka's autonomy and overrides her interests in favor of his own is precisely that used earlier by his family—language. As his relatives distribute the grandmother's possessions, the narrator remarks: "Seine Verwandten sprachen lebhaft durcheinander und er bemerkte, wie gut sie damit ihren Nutzen wahrten. Sie sprachen nicht schön, aber flink, hatten Mut zu ihrem Schwall, und es bekam schließlich jeder, was er wollte. Redenkönnen war nicht ein Mittel der Gedanken, sondern ein Kapital, ein imponierender Schmuck" (280). In contrast: "Wie stumm war Tonka. Sie konnte weder sprechen noch weinen" (280). The narrator in effect carries on the family's abusive practice by using language to form his myth, to accommodate Tonka to his need. In imagining her at this juncture (280) and later (304) as a "mitten in einem Sommertag allein niederfallende Schneeflocke," he denies her a place in a world bounded by natural laws and relegates her to a mythical realm that reflects his needs.

The fiction he creates finally does provide the narrator with a momentarily cohesive image. By narrating it, he creates a set of relations that define and delineate his subjectivity; he literally designs for himself a "raumzeitliche Anordnung," using Tonka as a pole of reference. Just as he had felt called upon to provide her with an image of her identity, he also needs her in order to discern his own image: "Er hätte ohne sie gar nicht gewußt, wie häßlich dieser Bart war, denn man weiß von sich so wenig, wenn man nicht andere hat, in denen man sich spiegelt" (295). Much like Ketten before he breaks out of his narcissistic shell, who sees in his wife's eyes only his own image, the narrator holds up the myth "Tonka" and seeks in it a reflection of himself. It is he, however, who brings coherence to the image; the structure of his discourse imposes provisional unity and closure on the fragmentary recollections of Tonka with which the narrative begins.

The "identity" the narrator attains is a construct of language, born of discourse. As such it lacks the permanent substantiality of the psychological "individual" or "self." Though neither determinately true nor tangibly fruitful, however, the myth of his identity does have an effect on the narrator/protagonist; his re-creation of Tonka's life effects a change in his own consciousness. His fiction does after all bring about a sense of "redemption"—the "kleiner warmer Schatten" he senses at certain moments—from the dissipation that unmitigated tension between faith and reason might have caused, but the "deliverance" remains momentary and fleeting.

The protagonist's inability to declare faith in Tonka has theoretical implications for the narrative. If the narrator reads Tonka's life and constructs a myth from this reading, the relation of his act of narration to his act of response should be examined. And given the fictional character as model, readers of the text might ask what implications they are offered by the images of reading and narrating, of subjective authority and interpretive response within it.

The adherence of Tonka's friend to the precepts of reason and science prevents him from establishing an absolute relationship to her, from accepting, in faith, "die Wahrheit ihrer Person" (295). Without faith, his mythic narrative remains on the plane of fiction, failing to attain the status of mythic truth (as it also foregoes the claims of epic prose, narrative certainty). The rational skepticism of Tonka's friend prevents his definitive understanding of her. No guarantee of truth, of "getting it right," supports her claim and his effort to read her. Forced to interpret and then respond accordingly, he becomes aware that he can never attain certitude, that no truth inheres in the events. Engaged in a task of interpreting the "signs" or "voices" of his life, he cannot accord authority to Tonka's person or to nonscientific possibilities. In this refusal he sets himself apart from interpreters in the hermeneutic tradition, rooted in Biblical exegesis, for whom the truth of the text is guaranteed by the divinity of its author. Having proudly rejected piety since childhood ("...denn er war schon klug und glaubte nicht" [300]), he cannot ground his myth in a metaphysical framework; instead he persists in his empirical approach.

The task of the narrator of "Tonka" resembles the task of the reader. Creation (construction) of the plot is shown to consist in reconstruction and revaluation. The product can never attain transparency or certainty but clearly remains an interpretation, a fictive image that calls attention to its fictivity. The narrator's discourse, which questions explicitly the relation between narrative and narrated events, the extensive use of similes, and the theme of despair at the impossibility of knowledge of the past highlight the dynamic and provisional quality of a narrative that ostensibly portrays a past event.

The narrative represents an act of reconstruction as defined by Iser. The reader approaches the text as the narrator of "Tonka" approaches the protagonist's experience; he creates a *Gestalt* by constructing a virtual world from the text, seeking consistency and unity in it and thereby imposing closure onto it. The text, however, constantly challenges the reader's image of the fictional world, jarring expectations by disclosing the illusory nature of the image as constructed. In identifying with the protagonist, the reader shares first the bewilderment and eventually the sense of redemption of Tonka's friend. Drawn to identification with the narrator, on the other hand, the reader adopts a reflective stance which undermines the illusion that had induced the initial identification. Above all, the reader shares the narrator's sense of urgency, the need to engage in the process of (re-)construction, despite uncertainty, to respond to the text as the narrator feels obliged to respond to Tonka. The narrator of "Tonka" essentially carries out the task described by Iser as that of readers: "We look forward, we look back, we decide, we change our decisions, we form expectations, we are shocked by their non-fulfillment, we question, we muse, we accept, we reject; this is the dynamic process of recreation" (68). The narrator of "Tonka" enacts the same dynamic, processual, and provisional strategy of reading.

An act of faith would have the effect of imposing closure on the plot of "Tonka," but, though it might resolve uncertainty, it would do so at the cost of intellectual honesty.[12] The modern reader, like Tonka's friend, is faced with the shortcomings of immanence and has no recourse to absolute metaphysical truth. Recognizing the absence of truth in or behind his object, the text, he must respond to it in some way or forego his involvement with it completely. The impossibility of faith impels him to accept a degree of responsibility.

The reader's responsibility thrusts him into the role traditionally associated with the subject of narration—that of agent. "Tonka" collapses the distinction between subjective and objective stance toward an object: Just as narrative subjectivity is shown to consist in interpretation, so too does reception come to entail authoritative or subjective initiation of action. Tonka's friend gains insight into the mutuality of activity and receptivity when he discovers that even simple perception depends not only on the reception of sensual stimuli but on a preceding action, for example an act of faith or assumption of unity and order:

> Er drückte seine Augen, sah umher, aber es waren nicht die Augen. Es waren die Dinge. Von ihnen galt, daß der Glaube an sie früher da sein mußte als sie selbst; wenn man die Welt nicht mit den Augen der Welt ansieht und sie schon im Blick hat, so zerfällt sie in sinnlose Einzelheiten, die so traurig getrennt voneinander leben wie die Sterne in der Nacht. (298)

The merging of authority and receptivity in this Novelle draws narrator and reader onto common ground, an area like that described by Musil as "Das Gebiet der Reaktivität des Individuums gegen die Welt und die anderen Individuen, das Gebiet der Werte und Wertungen, das der ethischen und ästhetischen Beziehungen, das Gebiet der Idee" (GW8 1028).

The place of "re-activity" in the concept of subjectivity and in the mediation carried out by the Novelle can be seen further in the problematic process of narration in "Die Amsel." Like the narrator of "Tonka," A2 desires to make sense of his past and test its truth by hearing it told. His result, however, falls short of that of Tonka's friend, allowing neither occasional insights into its truth, nor the comforting sensation of a "warm shadow"—a meaning, redemptive effect, or ever so subtle "conclusion." A2, narrator of his story, cannot fathom an end to it nor discern "den Sinn" (GW7 562). He feels himself to be a "good person" at the end of his narration, but he cannot say what a good person is.

The abrupt end to his narrative and his admitted inability to continue narrating or describing reenact the phenomenon that has closed each of the significant moments in his life—the condition of muteness, of having "verstummt." The word "verstummt" is reiterated after each episode. It refers first to the blackbird in Berlin, then to the *Fliegerpfeil*, and finally to the blackbird in the cage. Besides signifying the end of a perception of spiritual significance and a return to the mundane, it raises the question of interpretation of the apparently significant event preceding it, including how to react to it. When the harbinger of meaning becomes silent, the task of assigning meaning falls to the observer.

As a narration *of* narration, a story of a figure telling stories, "Die Amsel" at once demonstrates and thematizes the act of constructing a plot, a myth, to ascertain meaning. Though A2 poses as subject of his narrative, subjectivity is at stake rather than in control. A2 lacks authority to create a coherent narrative structure. If his story is to cohere as a *Gestalt*—a whole greater than the sum of the discrete episodes that constitute it—it can only be through the interpretive work of the recipient.

A2, who speaks most of the narration as a sort of "Selbstgespräch" (GW7 549)—a conversation with, about, and toward definition of the self—employs the fundamental narrative techniques of succession, parallelism, and repetition, in order to derive an aesthetic whole from, and thereby assert control over, the disparate events he relates. In recounting three occurrences that adhere in some ways to a common pattern, A2 tries to order them by contextualizing them and, through repetition, even ritualizing them. He tries to establish relation, *Zusammenhang*, and yet he worries, "Vielleicht habe ich unrecht, dir diese Geschichte im Zusammenhang mit zwei anderen zu erzählen, die darauf gefolgt sind" (553). In this and several other admissions of uncertainty, A2 demonstrates a point made by Martin Swales on the subjectivity characteristic of the Novelle. Swales concurs with most scholars of the genre that novellistic narrative is controlled and determined in a particular way by its subject, but he argues that the Novelle reveals inherent distrust of its own subjectivity.[13] A2 articulates the waning authority common to all the narrators of Musil's Novellen, and his uncertainty leads to collapse.

Whereas A2 has a serious and ambitious goal in telling his stories to A1, as indicated by his statement, "Ich will dir meine Geschichten erzählen, um zu erfahren, ob sie wahr sind;" (553), his telling produces no *Zusammenhang*, *Sinn* or truth value. In contradiction to M. L. Roth's claim that the narrative succeeds in synthesizing the events,[14] the text asserts their contingency: they simply happened.

Swales contends of the Novelle, that prosaic reality makes certain claims against subjectivity.[15] In A2's narrative, prosaic reality asserts itself so strongly over the attempt of a subject to master it that it refuses to yield to plotting or submit to a "raumzeitliche Anordnung." A2's experiences remain disordered, inscrutable, enigmatic: "Du lieber Himmel,—widersprach A2—es hat sich eben alles so ereignet; und wenn ich den Sinn wüßte, so brauchte ich dir wohl nicht erst zu erzählen" (562). The frustration with the narrative role expressed in this penultimate sentence carries over in the final statement to A2's frustration over his inability to function as an effective listener: "Aber es ist, wie wenn du flüstern hörst oder bloß rauschen, ohne das unterscheiden zu können" (562). Although there has been much discussion in the critical literature about the identity of the first narrator, A2, and A1 and their relation to each other,[16] it is clear that A2 and A1 are variants of the same subject whether or not their fictive pasts are identical. A2 engages in a conversation with A1 that can be told "fast wie ein Selbstgespräch" (549); "A" is both narrator and listener. The narrative is confessional in nature, and the figure who tells it conflates the two roles of a confession, carrying out both narrative and receptive functions. The story must be told *and* heard in order to achieve its purpose.

The frame narrator claims the importance of listening—the receptive function—for A2, reporting before the narration of the third episode, "Er schien unsicherer geworden zu sein, aber man konnte ihm anmerken, daß er gerade deshalb darauf brannte, sich diese Geschichte *erzählen zu hören*" (557, emphasis added). Several factors lend A2's narrative the character of a confession: the second person form of address, the professed need to narrate to another, the manner of narration *to* a listener "in der Art, wie man vor einem Freund einen Sack mit Erinnerungen ausschüttet, um mit der leeren Leinwand weiterzugehen," an image connoting penitential sackcloth (549), and the confessionals mentioned as a location for the friends' irreverent card games in their parochial school days (548). A2 insists to A1, after recounting how he came to abandon his wife, "Ich will übrigens nicht deine

Lossprechung" (553); but precisesly in denying the need for absolution, he raises suspicion of it.

Several of A2's comments, moreover, reveal a sense of guilt regarding his inability to respond appropriately to his parents and his wife. As in "Tonka," narrative purpose is tied to the question of response and responsibility. The parallel between the final images of confinement, even incarceration, of the Amsel in its cage and the childlike A2 in his room ("A"=Amsel?) cannot be overlooked.

A2, we know, was renowned as a youth for the "Kunststücke" executed "in schwindelnder Höhe" (GW7 548): one suspects that his narrative is his latest *Kunststück*, but one performed without his accustomed prowess. The final sentence, "Aber es ist, wie wenn du flüstern hörst oder bloß rauschen, ohne das unterscheiden zu können" (562) reveals the shortcoming of his narrative. It fails to cohere as meaningful language—"flüstern"—and cannot be distinguished from mere babble—"bloß rauschen." Perhaps as a result of his interpretive difficulties, A2 shows no greater readiness to respond to his third experience than to the two previous ones.

A2's narrative exhibits three dimensions in its purpose and, arguably, its insufficiency: In its inability to establish a *Zusammenhang*, to synthesize the three episodes into a coherent structure, the narrative exhibits aesthetic deficiency. When A2 and A1 fail to discern meaning in the narration, they reveal a hermeneutic shortcoming. Finally, the lack of a conclusion that would provide A2 with a basis for future actions ("das ist die dritte Geschichte, wie sie enden wird, weiß ich nicht" [562]), suggests an unresolved ethical dilemma.

Instead of having progressed to further action, A2 has regressed. He sits in the room where he spent his childhood, tending a caged bird, a reminder of mundane reality in contrast to the birds that appeared earlier as harbingers of heightened experience and expanded significance. In infantile obsession, A2 confuses this bird, now "verstummt," with the mother he neglected in her lifetime. Whereas Roth sees a productive tension between immanence and transcendence in the caging of the blackbird, the tendency toward lack of signficance and the absurdity of the end suggest, rather, regression from both transcendence and practical existence. A2's narrative fails to mediate between the natural and the fantastic, between prosaic reality and unheard-of events, as do traditional Novellen, including those of *Drei Frauen*. It also denies the experience of transcendence characteristic of the first two episodes of the story, while pushing to a perverse extreme A2's *Selbstsucht*, his obsessive but apparently futile effort at self-definition through narrative discourse. To an extent far greater than in "Tonka," the only completion to be attained in this Novelle must be executed by the reader.

The sense of insufficiency of A2's narrative in "Die Amsel" points retrospectively to the narrative purpose of all of Musil's Novellen. They are concerned with subjectivity, but neither in the Realistic sense of the preordained individual seeking his place in nature and society, nor in the Romantic sense of the immanent spirit striving toward union with a transcendent ego, nor in the sense of the subject in control of narration. Rather, subjectivity is determined by a set of relations, a structure or plot that is open to change motivated actively from within or in a receptive subject from outside itself. Yet its existence is posited and designed in the Novellen without the qualifying connotations of irony, as in the novel, or the generically tentative discursive speculations of the essay.

Musil's literary experimentation with subjectivity as relation anticipates in fiction the theoretical assertions of the linguist Emile Benveniste who posited subjectivity as a product of language that emerges in discourse from the opposition of the speaking subject to an other. "Tonka" and

"Die Amsel" present models of the relationship between subject, language, and discourse much like that proposed by Benveniste in *Problems in General Linguistics*. Rather than positing a preexistent subject manipulating language as an instrument to achieve a purpose, Benveniste argues that the subject actually comes into being through his use of language, specifically of the pronoun "I": "It is in and through language that man constitutes himself as a subject, because language alone establishes the concept of 'ego' in reality, in its reality, which is that of the being."[17] The subject, then, is a product of his discourse and of the language from which that discourse emerges.

The reader, too, in confronting and reconstituting the text, constructs a new subjectivity in relation to it, making of his act of reception an act of creation.[18] The text impels him to construct a subject, the subject of "his" thoughts as he reads. As he constructs this subject in relation to the rest of the narrative, he becomes himself the object of the discourse. "Die Amsel" assigns the task of creating subjectivity nearly completely to the reader, as first the frame narrator and then A2 abdicate their roles as controlling subjects of the narration.

In Musil's image of the individual as a "raumzeitliche Anordnung" (TB1 202) and of consciousness as "in einem Zusammenhang stehen" (TB1 202), and in the parallel between life and a narrative line drawn in "Vollendung der Liebe" (GW6 185), the existential dimension of narrative is affirmed. Narrative creates space for existence. The subject, in its various dimensions as consciousness, self, soul, or individual, is equated with space—a "Durchgangspunkt für Reflexionen" (GW8 1314) or an "unausfüllbarer Hohlraum im Raum" (GW6 215)—and the structure of fiction serves to delineate that space. Musil's Novellen thus continue to function as *exempla*, but in the sense of paradigms for existence, constellations of a subject open to change, *Gestalten* that can and will be transformed, rather than as particular examples of an absolute truth. While remaining open to variation, narrative discourse prevents dissolution of the self and is thus a crucial, though precarious, enterprise—the object of a struggle, "Kampf" (TB1 202). The flexibility, malleability, and dynamic nature of language accommodate it much better to the goals of the *Möglichkeitsmensch* than do the concrete actions characteristic of a *Tatmensch*, which are more likely to become stagnant and constrained, routinized into "seinesgleichen geschieht."

NOTES

1. WB 90f.

2. Wolfgang Kayser, *Entstehung und Krise des modernen Romans* (Stuttgart: Metzler, 1968) 34. Kayser claims, "Der Tod des Erzählers ist der Tod des Romans."

3. Wolfgang Iser, "Indeterminacy and the Reader's Response," in *Aspects of Narrative*, ed. J. Hillis Miller (New York: Columbia University Press, 1971) 12. See also *The Act of Reading* (Baltimore: Johns Hopkins University Press, 1978).

4. Roland Barthes, *S/Z*, tr. Richard Miller (New York: Hill and Wang, 1974) 4.

5. See Iser's works, op.cit.

6. Rudolf Otto, *The Idea of the Holy*, tr. John W. Harvey, 2nd ed. (London: Oxford University Press, 1957).

7. Susan Erickson, "The Psychopoetics of Narrative in Robert Musil's 'Die Portugiesin,'" *Monatshefte* 78 (1986) 2:167.

8. Rosmarie Zeller, "'Die Versuchung der stillen Veronika': Eine Untersuchung ihres Bedeutungsaufbaus," in *Sprachästhetische Sinnvermittlung: Robert Musil Symposion Berlin 1980*, hrsg. Dieter P. Farda und Ulrich Karthaus (Frankfurt and Bern: Lang, 1980) 135-153.

9. Brigitte Röttger, *Erzählexperimente: Studien zu Robert Musils 'Drei Frauen' und 'Vereinigungen'* (Bonn: Bouvier, 1973) 78.

10. Franz K. Stanzel, *Typische Formen des Romans* 3. Aufl., (Göttingen: Vandenhoeck & Ruprecht, 1967) 31.

11. Peter Henninger, "Schreiben und Sprechen: Robert Musils Verhältnis zur Erzählform am Beispiel von 'Drei Frauen' und 'Die Amsel,'" *Modern Austrian Literature* 9 (1976) 3/4: 57-99.

12. Walter H. Sokel, "Kleists 'Marquise von O.', Kierkegaards 'Abraham' und Musils 'Tonka': Drei Stufen des Absurden in seiner Beziehung zum Glauben," *Robert Musil: Studien zu seinem Werk*, hrsg. K. Dinklage, E. Albertsen, K. Corino (Hamburg: Rowohlt, 1970) 65.

13. Swales, 38.

14. Marie-Louise Roth, "'Die Amsel': Ein Interpretationsversuch," in *Robert Musil--Literatur, Philosophie, Psychologie*, hrsg. Josef und Johann Strutz, Musil-Studien 12 (München: Fink, 1984) 174.

15. See Swales, 34f.

16. See Henninger, "Schreiben und Sprechen..." and Karl Eibl, "Die dritte Geschichte: Hinweise zur Struktur von Robert Musils Erzählung 'Die Amsel,'" *Poetica* 3 (1970), 455-471. Also Peter Nutting, "Uncaging Musil's 'Amsel,'" *PMLA* 98 (1983) 1: 47-59.

17. Emile Benveniste, *Problems in General Linguistics*, tr. Mary Elizabeth Meek (Coral Gables: University of Miami Press, 1971) 224.

18. Norman N. Holland, "Unity Identity Text Self," in *Reader-Response Criticism: From Formalism to Post-Structuralism*, ed. Jane P. Tompkins (Baltimore: Johns Hopkins University Press, 1980) 118-133.

CHAPTER FIVE

Opportunities, Limits, and New Directions:
Robert Musil and the Novelle

After completing his first work of fiction, *Die Verwirrungen des Zöglings Törleß*, and having decided to pursue a career as a writer, Musil adopted the Novelle as the vehicle for his departure from the conventions of formal realism—the move he characterized as the "deutliche Wendung.... vom Realismus zu Wahrheit" (GW7 969). The choice may seem odd, as this genre is often mentioned in one breath with German literary realism of the nineteenth century. And the selection did lead to conflict with regard to matters of genre.

As Musil worked on his first Novellen he struggled against an inclination toward overly philosophical discourse. His Novellen, he felt, were in danger of becoming "zu sehr Essay" (T1 213), threatened by lifelessness and inflexibility. In an impulse, which produced at its extreme "Grigia" and "Die Portugiesin," Musil issued to himself the mandate: "Bilde, Dichter, rede nicht!" (GW8 1312). The novellistic convention of "objectivity," of veiling the subjective core of narrative in images of everyday life, seemed to offer him the possibility of cloaking philosophical ideas in the "ministeriellen Bekleidungsstücken" of mimetic form, which, pursued to an extreme, inevitably produced highly subjective, narcissistic myths that belie objectivity and subvert the mediation central to the Novelle.

In a 1912 essay on the Novelle, Musil calls attention to the propensity of the genre to focus on "das Problematische des Erzählens" itself: "So daß sich zeigt, was darin das Wesentliche sein soll; es handelt sich dann nicht mehr um ein Problem, sondern um das Problematische des Erzählens" (GW8 1323). Musil's reflection on his recently completed efforts in the genre, the *Vereinigungen*, anticipates the accomplishment of his future Novellen in presenting a variety of models for narration, specifically for the stance of a narrative subject in relation to the narrative. His statement utters an invitation, to be taken up in this final chapter, to examine the problem of narration and its resolution presented in each of Musil's Novellen.

The goal of this chapter is to determine how and why Musil's experiments with narrative and goals for literature converged with the traditional purpose of the Novelle and to describe the ways in which oeuvre and genre eventually diverged. Consistent with the dual focus of the project, the chapter will speculate on the direction taken by Musil's oeuvre with respect to genre and that taken by the generic tradition in the light of Musil's adaptations of it.

Musil addressed the genre Novelle directly in several essays, unpublished forewords, and in his diaries, some of which have been cited in Chapter One. He notes above all its degree of abstraction and propensity to distill the "inner form" of experience and embody it in narrative. The "truth" that he opposes to realism lies in the Novelle's power of limitation and allusion in contrast to the accomplishment of the novel—its direct and comprehensive statement: "Der Roman sagt aus u. sagt alles, die Novelle deutet an u. schränkt ein."[1] A statement from his journal that his first two Novellen "entfalten nicht, sie falten ein" (T1 350) conveys a similar conception of the connection between form and function specific to the Novelle and distinct from the novel. As the novel "unfolds" formally, it explicates; the Novelle, on the other hand, in folding in on itself, complicates.

In a "Vorwort" to the *Vereinigungen,* Musil connects this inclination of the Novelle toward "complication" with its task of setting forth and displaying its complex subject, in full relation to the whole and, as he writes, in full responsibility: "So hat man das Bedürfnis nach Sachen, die gewogen u geknetet u wieder gewogen u geknetet sind und in den leisesten Faltungen durchgeführt u in jedem Wort voll Beziehung zum Ganzen u voll Verantwortung sind, solche zu schreiben, wo man sich der Dichtung nur bedient um einiges herauszustoßen, hinzustellen, da sein zu lassen" (GW8 1312). His vision of the *Vereinigungen* echoes A. W. Schlegel's formulation that a well-told Novelle should not dissect its object but simply posit it, set it forth, and demand belief. The vision common to these two theorists of the Novelle upholds the power of nondiscursive, aesthetic language to show rather than imitate, analyze, or explain.

His statements on genre indicate that Musil recognized in the Novelle the convention of exemplification that informed the praxis—both production and reception—and the theory of the Novelle throughout its tradition. In facing the practical choice of genre that would command an expressive force lacking in realism, Musil turned to the convention according to which a Novelle is read as an *exemplum,* a paradigm, or parable, rather than as a description, analysis, or reflection.

 · The exemplary force of the Novelle incorporates both rational and affective faculties into the communicative act. Musil employed the Novelle to counter the limitations he saw in language. Through the Novelle, Musil responded to the dilemma of language skepticism in a manner consistent with the insights of the early Wittgenstein, and yet designed to transcend the limitations of language delineated by the philosopher. Based on a model of ordinary language and philosophical discourse, Wittgenstein declared in the *Tractatus* (1921) that ethical and aesthetic truths are unspeakable and thus consigned to the sphere of silence. Musil, however, employed the Novelle as a means, in Wittgenstein's formulation, to *show* what cannot be *said*.

The claim to exemplification of the Novelle tradition resonating in the statements by Musil cited above, points to the function of the genre within his oeuvre. The Novelle permits use of language to allude to "truths," to intimate insights. Its paradigmatic function draws on form to display knowledge that would become dogma—inflexible and therefore, from a modern perspective, invalid—if formulated discursively. It allows expression of a truth in a positive, albeit indirect, way, which, if systematically defined, could be expressed at best only negatively.

Each of the genres employed by Musil offers the potential to transcend the inadequacies of language, but the Novelle alone operates by means of this "exemplary" force, the product of "bilden," image-making. More than the other genres he adapts, the Novelle offers the formal potential to present examples, fragments of a "Lebenslehre in Beispielen" that Musil assumes as one of the tasks of literature: "Ich habe Dichtung einmal eine Lebenslehre in Beispielen genannt. Exempla docent. Das ist zuviel. Sie gibt die Fragmente einer Lebenslehre" (GW7 971).

The importance of the paradigmatic function of language—its power to "bilden" and "positiv hinstellen"—is underscored by the resemblance of its function as *exemplum* to the function of the stylistic device prominent in all of Musil's works, the *Gleichnis*. The frequency and importance of the *Gleichnis* in Musil's prose has been widely acknowledged,[2] but the common ground it shares in several important ways with the Novelle has remained unexamined until now.

The German word "Gleichnis"—"analogy" in a broad sense—subsumes both "metaphor" and "simile" in English. Musil's texts contain far more similes than metaphors, but both senses of the German word apply as I—along with Musil and his critics—use them here. The further possible English translation of *Gleichnis* as "parable" suggests *in nuce* the grounds for an analogy between the genre and the trope.

An analogy between Novelle and *Gleichnis*—form as genre and as style—can be drawn on the basis of function, of how meaning is constructed in the transaction between production and reception. The process by which the Novelle is realized on the level of the work mirrors the process incited by the *Gleichnis* at the level of the sentence. This process reveals a connection between the work and the metaphoric device on one hand and referents in the extratextual world on the other.

Both Novelle and *Gleichnis* attain meaning as act, as process, and thus transcend their content. The process of *Gleichnisbildung*, the realization of metaphoric meaning, involves both writer and reader. It consists in the recognition of similarity and difference between two phenomena, which reveals hitherto obscured aspects of both. Like the Novelle, the *Gleichnis* constitutes an interpretive act, triggered by an encounter with the unexpected, both for the subject of a narrative and for its recipient. Like the experience that Musil claims constitutes the Novelle, the realization of *Gleichnis* carried out by the reader is also an experience. At once receptive and creative, it is analogous to the Novelle as something that "breaks over" the writer ("über den Dichter hereinbricht" [GW9 1465]), and incites an act of interpretation that produces an aesthetic construction.

Novelle and *Gleichnis* thus similarly assign a receptive dimension to the creative role and a creative dimension to the act of reception.

The forms Novelle and *Gleichnis* offered Musil a means of integrating act and content in literature as his teacher Stumpf had attempted in his theoretical and methodological approaches to phenomenological psychology. The Novelle incorporates act and content by enacting, as it depicts, a hermeneutic venture in discourse. The result, the work, entails more than its mimetic content, that which it represents, connoting a larger meaning that is realized in the act of reading.

The operation by which metaphor establishes meaning incorporates both act and content into language. In his book, *The Rule of Metaphor,* Paul Ricoeur employs a territorial metaphor to depict the operation of figural language.[3] According to Ricoeur, metaphor is born of a "category mistake"; it oversteps the bounds of outworn classification and extends the "frontier" of customary usage—the "Sprache des Tags" (GW6 174) targeted by Musil—by bringing to light new connections and resemblances (197). Ricoeur's territorial metaphor for linguistic innovation echoes the phrase used by J. Schröder, "Grenzwert der Sprache,"[4] to denote Musil's goal of exploring the outermost bounds of language to renew stagnant and coopted forms of expression such as the formulaic language of "seinesgleichen geschieht" prevailing in "Kakania" in *Mann ohne Eigenschaften.*

In rupturing old forms, figural language reveals differences, transgressing the meaning signified by words in ordinary usage. It subverts the old meaning and creates a new connotation. The process is one of *Aufhebung,* by which the original meaning of the tenor is canceled but also preserved alongside the new connotation created by the juxtaposition of terms.

As Ricoeur points out, the simile most effectively preserves both terms by articulating both of them along with the comparative, "wie." It is, Ricoeur claims, the most intellectual of the forms of metaphor (186). Its intellectual straightforwardness accounts perhaps for its place in Musil's fiction, since it accommodates his goal of intellectual precision while also engaging the affective faculty. In explaining the appeal of Rilke's *Gleichnisse*, Musil praises their simultaneous intellectual and aesthetic accomplishment: "In allen solchen Fällen liegt der Reiz darin, daß ein schon etwas erschöpfter Gefühls- und Vorstellungsbereich dadurch aufgefrischt wird, daß ihm Teile eines neuen zugeführt werden. Das Tuch ist natürlich kein Novemberabend, diese Beruhigung hat man, aber es ist in der Wirkung mit ihm verwandt, und das ist eine angenehme kleine Mogelei" (GW8 1238). A use of language that communicates indirectly, calling attention to the "deception" it entails while causing pleasure, offers a potential solution to the dilemma created by the inadequacy of language.

A process of reordering similar to that of metaphor is set in motion in the Novelle on the level of the work as a whole. The unprecedented event represents a "category mistake" within the context of an accepted order, reality as it is commonly understood. The fictional work reshapes the accepted view by expanding and modifying it. The narration establishes a new relation between the apparently random, unusual, but "truest" (A. W. Schlegel) fact and reality as previously known and interpreted. The relation takes fictional shape in the literary work; the unique fact is not "explained away" or distorted to fit a preexisting system.

Ricoeur elucidates the realization of imagery in the act of reading by drawing on the Wittgensteinian concept of "seeing as" (212). By "seeing" one thing (a *Tuch*, to take the example from the speech on Rilke) "as" another (a

Novemberabend) in response to a verbal cue, readers imagine a point of view from which one is "as" the other. They recognize similarities and differences between the two terms of the comparison and recontextualize them in an intuitive (both intellectual and emotional) response. Ricoeur claims that the imaginative act of "seeing as" incited by metaphor establishes what he calls "metaphorical reference" between figural language and extratextual reality. He argues that the metaphor combines mimetic and mythic functions in a tension between a claim to referential truth ("the ontological vehemence of the metaphorical 'is'") and an awareness of the fictionality of the literary work ("the critical incision of the literal 'is not'" [252]).

In the field created by this tension between mimetic and mythic forces lie *Gleichnisse* as described by the narrator of *Mann ohne Eigenschaften*: "Ein Gleichnis enthält eine Wahrheit und eine Unwahrheit, für das Gefühl unlöslich miteinander verbunden" (GW2 581). The awareness of "untruth" calls attention to the trope as fictional construct (myth) rather than representation (mimesis), allowing expression of an alternative truth about the world to that suggested by the mimetic aspect of the fiction. The purpose of this function of metaphor as an interpretive act is described in Gérard Wicht's study of the *Gleichnis* in Musil's works. Wicht argues that metaphor fosters an understanding of the world as analogy, which forces us continually to see the world anew, to rewrite and reinterpret it. The *Gleichnis* is the medium that demands interpretation and makes knowledge possible. It is the hermeneutic instrument of knowledge of the world.[5] Revision also often demands new and creative response.

Ricoeur's concept of "seeing as" elucidates the exemplary function of the Novelle. In its hermeneutic challenge—bringing an unusual event into confrontation with an accepted order—the Novelle incites the reader to "see" reality in a new way, "as" the world of the work. To an extent, all fiction invites such re-vision of reality, but the Novelle, like metaphor, does so by way of exemplification, presenting in a deictic manner what in other genres is represented descriptively or analytically. In addition, the Novelle thematizes the process it enacts, creating a new image of a given view and expanding the conventional order to accommodate the exception. In the new light shed upon it, to borrow the metaphor from the theories of Tieck and Ernst, an event acquires fresh significance and value, as does the order with which it is aligned. To cite Musil's own examples, an ordinary act of infidelity becomes a perfection of love, separation leads to a more intense union, the dissipation of life is valued as a release from bondage, the death of a small cat signals a miraculous salvation, or the death of a young woman produces something that, according to the narrator of "Tonka," made him better than others.

The secondary reference delineated by Ricoeur that accounts for the force of the Novelle as *exemplum* provides a theoretical foundation for the connection between aesthetic and ethical purpose that Musil claims for art. It implicitly contradicts the claims of scholars, for example Liliane Weißberg,[6] who attribute a radical aestheticism to Musil's works, or assert their existence as complete and independent "totalities" reflecting a pure "Zuständlichkeit" of the self, such as Hans Schaffnit.[7] The exemplary function of the Novelle and the *Gleichnis* affirms Musil's characterization of the "Heimatgebiet des Dichters" as a combined aesthetic and ethical territory: "das Gebiet der Reaktivität des Individuums gegen die Welt und die anderen Individuen, das Gebiet der Werte und Bewertungen, das der ethischen und ästhetischen Beziehungen, das Gebiet der Idee" (GW8 1028). This mutuality of aesthetic and ethical concerns in Musil's essays has been elucidated by Roth, and the association between response and responsibility within the Novellen argued in my Chapter Four offers further intertextual evidence of the connection between these two concerns in Musil's oeuvre.

Musil comes close to expressing the concept of "seeing as" in the essay "Novelleterlchen." He claims that the significance of an experience stems from a shift in context, attained when it is viewed under new categories of thought: "Wo uns ein Mensch erschüttert und beeinflußt, geschieht es dadurch, daß sich uns die Gedankengruppen eröffnen, unter denen er seine Erlebnisse zusammenfaßt...." (GW8 1326). The exemplification achieved by the forms Novelle and *Gleichnis* allows such a re-vision of experience by inciting the reader to see reality "as" the fictional world of a work. The combined mythic-mimetic process synthesizes the mythic potential of artistic construction and the mimetic impulse toward representation of experience (inner and outer) in literature.

One of the main problems presented to a modernist sensibility by the function of the Novelle as *exemplum* is closure. A generic convention of closure would seem to contradict the claim of Musil's theoretical texts that literature opens possibilities and liberates "truth" from the causal and logical connections of language in conventional usage. Aesthetic closure implies system, a general order from which particular phenomena derive significance, as in the concept of fate in ancient tragedy, the Aristotelian concept of cosmic order, or the Hegelian notion of History. According to these views, particular examples possess meaning and value by rendering an absolute truth in visible form. This view of closure dominates the view of the Novelle in the nineteenth and early twentieth centuries.[8]

Despite the closure of its compact form, Musil actually appropriates the Novelle for the task of opening possibilities, "Möglichkeiten in Seelen hineinbohren"

(GW8 1317). He reverses the significance attributed to aesthetic closure by Aristotle and Hegel that had marked the Novelle in the era of realism. Musil's literary and discursive writings proclaim the importance of formal closure as an antidote to the dissolution and anarchy in individual experience, language, science, and culture. His Novellen represent tentative syntheses, provisional hedges against the threat of literary and cultural decadence of the *fin de siècle*. Rather than reflecting the eternal truth of a permanent, determinate order or inevitable course of history, they make visible structural relations that give shape to existence. They provide a means of self-definition for individuals, nations, and cultures that is impossible when these entities are regarded as isolated and random phenomena or as fixed substances subject to regulation by external forces. Relation is more significant to identity than is essence, Musil asserts in "Der deutsche Mensch als Symptom" (1923): "Es zeigt sich, daß die Frage des europäischen Menschen: was bin ich? eigentlich heißt: wo bin ich? Es handelt sich nicht um die Phase eines gesetzlichen Prozesses und nicht um ein Schicksal, sondern einfach um eine Situation. Gesetze vermöchte man nicht zu ändern; Situationen in diesem Sinn aber wohl...." (GW8 1375).

With this phenomenology of relation, in contrast to that of analysis into discrete elements, Musil suggests a framework for a concept of closure that would replace the *Totalitätsgedanke* of the Novelle of the nineteenth century with a more consistently modernist concept. By way of the branch of phenomenology that focuses on act and its continuation in *Gestalt* theory, Musil opens the theoretical framework of the Novelle by introducing a notion of provisional, dynamic closure. With provisional closure, a literary work, as also experience, acquires structure, but it proclaims no particular *Weltanschauung* as original or final truth. A view of closure as a coherent, but changeable form, one of many possibilities, open at any moment to reconstruction, is Musil's legacy to the Novelle tradition. His works draw out a potential that had existed inherently but dormantly in the tradition, making explicit the "modernity" often attributed—without explanation—to the genre.

The Novelle as genre had been well disposed to a notion of *Gestalt*. The novellistic problem emerges from disruption of an initial order—what Musil called in the context of an essay on film "die Sprengung des normalen Totalerlebnisses" (GW8 1145)—and produces a new constellation that acknowledges the exceptional instance. Viewed as *Gestalt*, the Novelle accomplishes "die Zusammenfassung zu einem neuen Zusammenhang," which, instead of locating the universal in the particular, entails as much an expansion of impressions as a reduction (GW8 1139).

Musil's Novellen illustrate the process of "Sprengung" followed by a "Zusammenfassung zu einem neuen Zusammenhang" that entails some degree of closure. In "Vollendung der Liebe" Claudine's act of adultery attains meaning and value only within a particular set of relations—her marriage and past experiences. The importance of relation is highlighted in the geometric images of the opening scene, most particularly that of the structural member of an edifice, the "Strebe aus härtestem Metall" (GW6 156) with which the bond between Claudine and her husband is compared. The question of inner motivation, a particular form of relation, is raised in this Novelle in connection with the legal and ethical question of accountability in the case of the (doubly) fictional character G. After discussing these questions with her husband within the context of a discussion of their relationship, Claudine breaks away from the situation that has defined her existence and enters a strange environment where she establishes a new liaison.

Within the narrative framework she reconstructs the shape of her existence and invests her past relationship with fresh significance and value. The new set of relations offers no more permanence than the last, reveals no absolute "fate," but it demarcates the parameters of Claudine's existence in a way that an unstructured flux of experience would not. In addition, the narrative evokes in the reader the sense of a "message," however unsystematic and ambiguous it may be.

In "Versuchung der stillen Veronika," the protagonist follows a similar course. She escapes the confinement of her aunt's house vicariously, experiencing a sense of release and expansion as Johannes travels to the sea and, she supposes, to his death. She then reestablishes a sense of order, a renewed sense of relation (*Zusammenhang*) to her surroundings on the following day.

"Grigia" and "Die Portugiesin" exhibit a far greater degree of closure than the *Vereinigungen*. The "worlds" conjured by these texts are dream-worlds reflecting a narcissistic condition. When the "objective" world can be identified as a projection of subjective forces—the complex of needs and desires of a psyche—the text achieves a closure whose terms are satisfaction of the lack suffered by the controlling psyche. In its hermetic enclosure from a realistic setting, the fictional world consists nearly exclusively in relation—of the protagonist to a place (foreign and familiar) and to a female counterpart.

In "Tonka" and "Die Amsel" the subjective authority creating the structural relations comes to the fore, drawing attention to the difficulty of attaining closure, of creating even a temporary *Gestalt*, through narrative discourse. The narrators of these Novellen experience in increasing measure "das Problematische des Erzählens." Exposure of the precariousness of their authority strains the limits of the Novelle for Musil.

"Die Amsel" portrays the attempt of A2 to construct a cohesive vision of his experience, to "see" it "as" a coherent whole. A2's narrative task is "bilden"—forming, plotting, myth-making. In conjunction with the frame narrator, whose voice recedes as the narrative progresses, A2 crafts a plot which, by creating a meaningful image of three significant episodes from his life, would define his identity. A2 struggles to construct a paradigm, to define a nexus of relations that would constitute his "Bewußtsein," which Musil defined in a journal entry as "in einem Zusammenhang stehen" (T1 452). A2 emphasizes the need for both narrating and listening in this process of self-determination; only in hearing himself telling his story does he hope to ascertain its sense. The reader is called upon to reenact the narrative process—the combined activity of narration, interpretation, and evaluation—left uncompleted by both narrators in the text.

A2's internal narration and the opening "frame" narrative converge at the close. The absence of the frame at the end brings the moment of enunciation into the foreground. This focus on the act of narrating and its uncertainty breaks the novellistic frame and prevents closure, opening the work onto its context, the storytelling situation. A2's attempt at "bilden" fails to yield a tightly structured and hermetic myth like those of *Drei Frauen*.

The experiences A2 wants to understand and evaluate (in order to ascertain their implications for the present "story" of his life) assert their independence of an interpretive framework. A2 remains unable to integrate his experiences into a narrative line. He finds himself in a dilemma like that perceived by Claudine in "Vollendung der Liebe" when, comparing coherent language with meaningful continuity in an individual life, she notes, "man fürchtet, im Augenblick des abreißenden Schweigens irgendwie unvorstellbar zu taumeln und von der Stille aufgelöst zu werden; aber es ist nur Angst, nur Schwäche vor der schrecklich auseinanderklaffenden Zufälligkeit alles dessen, was man tut" (GW6 185). A2 is faced with the contingency ("die auseinanderklaffende Zufälligkeit") of his life experience. He cannot satisfy his listener's expectation that he know the meaning of his narrative in advance. He can only restate the facticity of his experience: "es hat sich eben alles so ereignet" (GW7 562). He thus encounters the limitations of the power of "bilden" to establish meaning or "truth."

The outcome of A2's attempt at "bilden" are three experiences that "simply happened." In an Aristotelian sense he is left with history—the raw data of experience (as he remembers it)—with no unified structure, no *mythos* to lend it the force of truth. The tentativeness of his endeavor to construct a mythic image from the material of his life becomes evident. The necessity informing Aristotelian mythos is lacking. A2 has recourse to no origin or end, no cosmic totality to authenticate his story. He must establish his own terms of closure, but these elude him; they become the task of the reader.

In the absence of closure, accentuated by the abdication of the frame narrator and A2's claim, "wie sie [die Geschichte] enden wird, weiß ich nicht" (GW7 562), "Die Amsel" returns discourse (*reden*) to the foreground of the Novelle, exposing the source of the narrative in a discursive act of a speaking subject. Rather than cloaking or concealing itself in "ministerielle Bekleidungsstücke," as in "Grigia" and "Die Portugiesin," the controlling "subjektive Stimmung und Ansicht" at the core of the Novelle is brought forward from its place of concealment.

The conventional goal of novellistic discourse, the act of mediation attempted by A2, is exposed in Musil's last Novelle as highly subjective, not with the effect of dismissing it as inauthentic or false but of affirming the need for it: "wenn ich den Sinn wüßte, so brauchte ich dir nicht erst zu erzählen" (GW7 563). The urgency of expression, the "Seelennot" averred by Emerson, and by Musil in quoting him, to pervade public and private existence (T1 170), becomes for A2 a nearly desperate need on aesthetic, hermeneutic, and ethical levels. He struggles on the aesthetic plane to attain closure by completing his story, on the hermeneutic plane to ascribe meaning to it, and, on the ethical, to address its implications for present and future action, that is, to finish the story as narrated time converges with narrative time at the end. He tries to piece together a "Lebenslehre" from discrete, impressionistic experiences by transforming them into "Beispiele," something he can accomplish only by investing them with meaning.

The uncertainty of A2's narrative illustrates the limitations of the dictum noted in the foreword to the *Vereinigungen*: "Bilde, Dichter, rede nicht!" "Die Amsel" reflects a strain on the form of the Novelle and thus points to its limits. A2's inability to construct a coherent image, to attain closure (other than the mockery thereof in the final images of confinement of the Amsel in the cage and the man in the child's room), suggests extension of the formal potential of the genre to its limits. While pointing to the difficulty of investing experience with meaning, of creating "Beispiele" by the process of "bilden," Musil succeeded in creating an image, an *exemplum*, of the narrative process and in marking the outer boundaries of the Novelle.

The shift in emphasis from *bilden* in *Vereinigungen* and *Drei Frauen* to *reden* in "Tonka" and "Die Amsel" results from a shift in the nature of the subject-object relation. In the unconventional but mimetic mode of the *Vereinigungen*, as we have seen, the narrator assumes the role of scientific observer and recorder of psychic activity. Language, especially metaphor, serves to compensate for the expressive shortcomings of scientific notation. The relation of the narrator to the characters is motivated by curiosity about the workings of the mind. The narrators of these Novellen play a role resembling that of Törleß in Musil's early novel, who tells Basini, the object of his intense observation: "Ich wollte einen Punkt finden, fern von dir, um dich von dort anzusehen..., das war mein Interesse an dir...." (GW6 124). Like Törleß they are motivated by fascination with psychic processes and seek to capture them in language.[9]

In "Grigia" and "Die Portugiesin," by contrast, where the perspective and voice of the narrators cannot be distinguished from those of the protagonists, the controller of discourse, the power wielding language and thus shaping the fictional world, is masked. The reader is drawn into a stylized, artificial world which, despite initial gestures toward realism, is structured by categories of a unitary consciousness. The technique of *bilden* to which Musil had recourse in order to avoid excessive analytical discourse yields in these works narcissistic structures that preclude representation of external reality. The "subjektive Stimmung and Ansicht" controlling the narrative remains "verhüllt" and "verborgen."

Unlike Musil's former and subsequent Novellen and many in the tradition, these stories have no frame. Whereas the Novelle conventionally acknowledges the act of mediation by specifying the narrative situation in a frame, "Grigia" and "Die Portugiesin" erase traces of subjectivity. More than the other Novellen, these mythic works hide their character as spoken/written discourse. The relations they embody—of the male protagonist to his surroundings and to his female counterpart—are portrayed as objectively realistic.

In "Tonka" and "Die Amsel" the subjective force engaged in construction, in the process of *bilden*, is made explicit. Breaking the hermetic seal around the image opens it onto the present of the narrative act and reveals its character as *reden*. In expressing the problems of remembering and forgetting, of reconstructing the past from a moment in the present, "Tonka" draws the Novelle convention of specifying the narrative situation in a frame to its logical conclusion. Although the mythic structure of the first two works of *Drei Frauen* informs "Tonka" as well, in "Tonka" the myth is exposed as a fictional construct, a "Märchen" with the potential to impede or obstruct, even to hurt, as suggested by the metaphor "Dornengerank." The myth of "Tonka" is clearly a human construct, a difficult attempt at interpreting and reconciling past events, which cannot compel belief.

In "Tonka" as in "Die Amsel" the illusion of the story is interrupted by the discourse of the narrator, for example in his query, "Aber war es überhaupt so gewesen? Nein, das hatte er sich später zurechtgelegt" (GW6 270). In questioning the accuracy of the narrative, these interruptions call attention to discourse as speech, as a process—creating and created by a subject—rather than a formed whole (*Gestalt*). In so doing, they signal a return in Musil's oeuvre to *reden*, as opposed to *bilden*. Despite his earlier fears that his fiction became "zu sehr Essay" as he departed from realistic conventions, Musil later departs from the Novelle and returns to essayistic discourse—*reden*.

In the latter part of his career Musil used genres that allow explicitly discursive—openly conceptual and analytical—use of language. Turning from images or paradigms that "positiv hinstellen," he takes up forms that "motivirend zergliedern." One of these is the essay; the other is the novel.

Musil wrote essays in the years when he was also producing the Novellen (1908-1928). He explored the possibilities of these genres—of "bilden" and "reden" respectively—as parallel alternatives for expression. In experimenting with these forms, he defined them in opposition to each other. The importance he attached to the Novelle at this time may thus be explained by the drawbacks of the essay as he saw it. In an unpublished fragment written in 1910 Musil compares the essay with other genres on the basis of a joint appeal to the intellect and the emotions:

> Jede Novelle jeder Roman u jedes Drama hat ein "Problem" ...Dieses Problem könnte im Essay behandelt werden. Es muß im Leben jedes großen Dichters od. Kritikers den zufälligen Punkt geben, wo er der eine oder der ander würde. Das Problem im Essay behandelt wäre ermüdend, schleppend. Es ist der Augenblick der gedanklichen Unheiligkeit, des Handwerks, wenn man sich zur Vivisicirung entschließt ...Man spricht Gedanken im Roman od. in der Novelle nicht aus sondern läßt sie anklingen. Warum wählt man dann nicht lieber den Essay? Eben weil diese Gedanken nichts rein Intellektuelles sind sondern ein Intellektuelles verflochten mit Emotionalem. Weil es mächtiger sein kann solche Gedanken nicht auszusprechen sondern zu verkörpern ...Die Suggestivkraft der Handlung ist stärker als die des Gedankens. (GW8 1300f)

This passage expresses fear that conceptual discourse will lose its vitality, discussed also in the essayistic sketch, "Über Robert Musil's Bücher." The difficulty of integrating thought and emotional impact in one form may explain Musil's exploration of two distinct generic forms in the subsequent decade.

In an essay of 1913, Musil distinguishes between the essay as a finished written product and a general essayistic mode of thought that later became the "Utopie des Essayismus" to which the character Ulrich of *Mann ohne Eigenschaften* devotes himself (GW1 247ff). This utopian state (of mind) gains more adequate expression in the novel than in works of the essay genre itself. While "essayistisches Denken" remains receptive, dynamic, and open to change, the written form runs the risk of stagnation and petrifaction into system.

The essay, Musil wrote, has its form and method from science and its material from art. It tries to create an order. Rather than giving an image, it connects thoughts logically, beginning with facts, like science, and sets them in relation" (GW8 1335). "Essayistic thinking" allows perception by direct intuition akin to mystical experience, but the essay itself excludes mysticism and pretense to knowledge. It carries out a didactic task: "Wir scheiden nun die mystischen Interessen aus, weil ihr Gegenstand metaphysisch ist und weil sie eine Erkenntnis prätendieren, während wir für den Essay nur menschliche Umbildung beanspruchen" (GW8 1337).

Though it asserts logical order, the essay does not, according to this view, display the closure of the Novelle, leaving the Novelle the task of creating integral relations not captured in the "Zwitterreizen des Essays" (GW8 1317). The Novelle, in contrast to the essay, avoids the tendency toward systematization. In its nature as provisional *Gestalt*, it is not bound to a logical or dogmatic order. The improbable event depicted in the Novelle explicitly defies schematization and hence requires mediation to establish new relations and permit understanding.

The exemplary function of the Novelle permits a synthesis of intellectual and aesthetic powers and provides an opportunity for expression distinct from the essay. And yet, as we have seen, Musil's Novellen gradually expose their nature as discourse, undermine their paradigmatic illusion, and reveal themselves as precarious discursive undertakings resisting closure. Intellectual honesty about the impossibility of simply "setting forth" and demanding acceptance leads Musil back to the essay, where the written word is more closely identified with the speech of the author, and to the novel, which presents many "voices" but, often through irony, makes clear the "subjectivity" of the standpoint from which each voice speaks. The myriad of possibilities presented by the novel renders it the best form to embody the "essayism" to which Musil turned when he had exhausted the possibilities of the Novelle for his literary enterprise. Susan Lanser expresses the rich potential of the novel in her book *The Narrative Act*: "The novel emerges from the beginning as a multi-systemic form with the capacity to integrate virtually any mode of discourse within its frame, to tell one story or a dozen and to create as many tellers as tales, to reproduce both written and oral documents, and to define within a broad spectrum of possibilities its relationship to history."[10] In *Mann ohne Eigenschaften* Musil pursues many of the options Lanser identifies. He integrates many modes of discourse with a "subject" that serves as a lens/voice observing, describing, and reflecting from a roving perspective. The result is not a *Gestalt* but rather a labyrinth, the various avenues of which are explored.

The voice that articulates the visions maintains an ironic tone. Operating only by an imposed discrepancy between what is said and the motivation behind it, irony calls attention to the moment of enunciation and thus to the arbitrariness of the discourse. Musil asserts the appeal of irony as a mode of expression: "Während der rund 10 [ersten] Manuskripte zu dem ersten 200 Seiten des MoE: Die bedeutungsvolle Selbsterkenntnis, daß die mir gemäße Schreibweise die der Ironie sei. Gleichbedeutend mit dem Bruch mit dem Ideal der Schilderung überlebensgroßer Beispiele....Gleichbedeutend auch mit der Erkenntnis, daß ein Dichter nicht bis zum philosophischen System vordringen soll (u. kann)" (T1 928). Musil's departure from "positive" signification and move to the "negative" modes of irony and deferral of meaning are indicated in his

admiring commentary on a book by Alfred Polgar entitled
An den Rand geschrieben. His anticipation of postmodern
concepts of language such as marginality, deferral,
including the gesture of crossing out the written word,
dissemination (*Auflösung*), supplementarity (*Zusätze*),
and codes (*Durchführungsbestimmungen*), becomes clear in
Musil's claim that Polgar's book introduces "die Dichtung
der Zukunft":

> [er] schreibt darin der Seele des zeitgenössischen
> Menschen, die bekanntlich allgemein schmerzlich
> vermißt wird, kleine, unpathetische Bemerkungen
> an den Rand; wenn man zur Mitte hinblickt, wo sie
> sein müßte, ist alles durchstrichen und es bleibt dort
> nichts, aber in der Randkorrektur, den Fußnoten,
> dem Dolchstoß praktischer Betrachtung in den
> Rücken der poetischen, in dieser sich immer tiefer
> zerspaltenden Heterodoxie der Vorbehalte,
> scheinbar also in einer unheilbaren Auflösung,
> zeigen sich mit einemmal ihre Linien; denn auch das
> Leben hat heute keinen Text, sondern nur Zusätze,
> Einschränkungen, Durchführungsbestimmungen und
> jeden Tag neue Novellierungen, vale Ehrwürdiges,
> was uns lieb war, dankt ab: aber das Leben war wohl
> immer die sozusagen konstituierende Auflösung einer
> Versammlung. (GW8 1159)

The compact form of the Novelle would indeed be too
limited a vehicle for this contemporary soul. Musil
himself took a giant practical step toward initiating the
Zukunftsdichtung anticipated in his theoretical comment
on Polgar's book.

Although Musil pursued other genres, "Tonka" and
"Die Amsel" suggest a model for a viable "Novellentyp
des zwanzigsten Jahrhunderts."[11] These Novellen
demonstrate the difficulty and the ethical uncertainty of

assigning meaning to life through narrative. They cast into relief the tension between subjective and objective "reality" and also the task of mediating between them, accentuating both the urgency and the difficulty of the enterprise. Though they refrain from masking the subjective source of narrative in objective images, these Novellen nonetheless mediate between the claims of apparently random realistic occurrences and the desires of a subjective consciousness for coherence. The challenge to the subject to define himself by plotting a position relative to objects and events outside his consciousness, to acknowledge and represent the facticity of objective phenomena, and yet to define a relation to them, no matter how precarious, suggests a model for later Novellen.

In pointing to the joint enterprise of narrator and reader, an undertaking that has both a creative, active dimension and a receptive, interpretive component, Musil's Novellen assert their modernity. According to Barthes' distinction between modern and traditional literature, these are "writerly" texts,[12] in that they encourage the reader to engage in (re-)construction, (re)writing. At the same time, however, though not "readerly" in Barthes' sense, they nevertheless ask to be read. In highlighting the difficulty and urgency of receptivity, interpretation, and response, they demand response (responsiveness and responsibility) to extratextual reality on the part of both writer and reader.

Such a delineation of possibilities for a modern Novelle remains just that—a sketch of possibilities. It in no way asserts prescriptive limitations on the genre. Nor does it claim to supersede a descriptive approach that would survey short prose written in this century with an aim of identifying novellistic tendencies. These might be found, for example, in the short prose of Ingeborg Bachmann, but an actual investigation of her works and those by other authors extends beyond the parameters of the present study.

It is nonetheless useful, I feel, to chart the territory we have seen opened by Musil's Novellen for a modern Novelle. The two central aspects of the Novelle set forth in the foregoing chapters would be present in modern novellistic texts—a tension between subjectivity and objectivity and a claim to exemplify truth in some way. Works encompassing these concerns would stand apart from the short story in maintaining the subject-object tension that defines the unique interpretive relationship to the world constituted by the Novelle. Interpretation entails contextualization and thus differs from the purpose of the short story—to isolate a moment of experience and present it as a fragmentary "slice of life" with no necessary beginning or end and little sense of embeddedness in or relation to a broader range of existence.

The criterion of tension between subject and object would also exclude short prose that portrays no clash of worlds necessitating an interpretive act. Fiction that is either so highly subjective as to constitute a private, fantastic world with no claim to public interest, or, on the other hand, so highly objective as to obscure the subjective endeavor to make sense and accord value would fall outside the realm of the Novelle. Finally, the modern Novelle would be concerned with asserting a "true," that is, a convincing and commonly acceptable interpretive image of the relation between an unusual phenomenon and a general understanding.

The modernity of this post-Musilian Novelle would consist in the openness with which the interpretive act is acknowledged. No longer disguising the subjective source of control in order to maintain illusion, a modern Novelle, taking "Tonka" as an example, would call attention to its source in a discursive act with specific motivation, the problematic aspect of such an act—"das Problematische des Erzählens"—and the constructedness of its story. It would also, as in "Tonka" and most extremely in "Die Amsel" construct a larger space for the reader and thereby alter the concept of subjectivity from that of a single controlling consciousness to that of a process of signification and interpretation carried out in the transaction between narrator and reader. It would thus acknowledge the common, meaningful enterprise of a narrator whose narration constitutes a reading and a reader who becomes subject and must construct the narrative if it is to be realized.

Such a modern Novelle would present a natural outgrowth of the Novelle of the nineteenth century.[13] But it would occupy the opposite end of a spectrum spanning the distance between the goals of narrowing a vision of the world in order to cope with it and expanding the vision to make room for new possibilities. More so than the typical, it would portray an exceptional instance, but one compelling interpretation and response in a large readership. And it would present a narrative construct not as particular example of an absolute totality—a parabolic image within the framework of dogma—but rather as a provisional Gestalt—a fragment of a Lebenslehre that by definition cannot become a closed, universal system.

NOTES

1. In Roth, 468f.

2. Jürgen Schröder published the first, detailed study of metaphoric language in his article, "Am Grenzwert der Sprache: Zu Robert Musils 'Vereinigungen,'" Euphorion 60 (1966) 311-334. Other studies of Gleichnisse have focused

on *Mann ohne Eigenschaften*, including a recent work that was helpful to me, Gérard Wicht, *'Gott meint die Welt keineswegs wörtlich'*: *Zum Gleichnisbegriff in Robert Musils Roman 'Der Mann ohne Eigenschaften,'* Europäische Hochschulschriften 792 (Bern: Lang, 1984).

3. Paul Ricoeur, *The Rule of Metaphor: Multidisciplinary Studies of the Creation of Meaning in Language*, tr. Robert Czerny (Toronto: University of Toronto Press, 1981).

4. Schröder, 311-334.

5. Wicht, 133.

6. Liliane Weißberg, "Versuch einer Sprache des Möglichen: Zum Problem des Erzählens bei Robert Musil," *Deutsche Vierteljahresschrift* 54 (1980) 464-484.

7. Hans Wolfgang Schaffnit, *Mimesis als Problem: Studien zu einem ästhetischen Begriff der Dichtung aus Anlaß Robert Musils* (Berlin: de Gruyter, 1971).

8. For example, in comparing it to the drama, Theodor Storm claimed the Novelle required "die geschlossenste Form" (WB 72), and Ernst wrote, "Die Novelle ist, wie die Drama, eine abstrahierende Kunstform; sie gibt nicht Breite und Fülle durch Zufälligkeit des scheinbaren Lebens, sondern sie gibt das Notwendige und erzielt ihre Wirkung durch Geschlossenheit und strenge Fügung."

9. The entire passage from *Törleß* explicitly associates the pose of distanced observer with the task of committing what is observed to language: "Früher glaubte ich immer, daß ich für dich ein Wort, eine Empfindung finden müßte, die dich anders bezeichnete; aber es gibt wirklich nichts

Bezeichnenderes, als zu sagen, daß du schlecht und feig bist. Das ist so einfach, so nichtssagend und doch alles, was man vermag. Was ich früher anderes von dir wollte, habe ich vergessen, seit du dich mit deinen geilen Bitten dazwischen gedrängt hast. Ich wollte einen Punkt finden..." (GW6 124).

10. Susan Sniader Lanser, *The Narrative Act: Point of View in Prose Fiction* (Princeton: Princeton University Press, 1981) 109f.

11. Fischer, 236. In her article on Musil's concept of the novelle, Fischer designates as the task of further scholarship on the novelle a definition of a twentieth-century type, which would have to be distinguished above all from other short forms.

12. Barthes, *S/Z*, 4.

13. In Martini's important article on the Novelle in bourgeois realism, he makes it clear that the genre was not used merely to isolate and thereby simplify experience, nor was the Novelle made to reflect such an ordered cosmos to the extent that is often claimed. The tendency to problematize "reality" emerged increasingly toward the end of the nineteenth century.

BIBLIOGRAPHY

Primary Works

Musil, Robert. *Gesammelte Werke in neun Bänden.* hrsg. Adolf Frisé. 2. Aufl. Hamburg: Rowohlt, 1981.

---------- *Beiträge zur Beurteilung der Lehren Machs.* Hamburg: Rowohlt, 1980.

---------- *Briefe 1901-1942.* hrsg. Adolf Frisé. Hamburg: Rowohlt, 1981.

---------- *On Mach's Theories.* tr. Kevin Mulligan, intro. G. H. von Wright. München, Wien: Philosophia Verlag, 1982.

---------- *Tagebücher.* hrsg. Adolf Frisé. Hamburg: Rowohlt, 1976.

Secondary Works

Adorno, Theodor. "Standort des Erzählers im zeitgenössischen Roman." *Noten zur Literatur I.* Frankfurt: Suhrkamp, 1974, 61-73.

Aristotle. *Poetics*. In Potts, L.J. *Aristotle on the Art of Fiction: An English Translation of Aristotle's 'Poetics.'* Cambridge: Cambridge University Press, 1968.

Arntzen, Helmut. Satirischer Stil: *Zur Satire Robert Musils in 'Mann ohne Eigenschaften.'* Bonn: Bouvier, 1960.

Bangerter, Lowell A. *Robert Musil*. New York: Continuum, 1989.

Barthes, Roland. "The Death of the Author." In *Image, Music, Text*. Ed. and tr. Stephen Heath. New York: Hill and Wang, 1977.

---------- *S/Z*, Tr. Richard Miller. New York: Hill and Wang, 1974.

Benveniste, Emile. *Problems in General Linguistics*. Tr. Mary Elizabeth Meek. Coral Gables: University of Miami Press, 1971.

Berger, Peter. "Robert Musil and the Salvage of the Self," *Partisan Review*, 51 (1984) 639-651.

Berghahn, Wilfried. *Robert Musil*. Hamburg: Rowohlt, 1963.

Boring, Edward G. *A History of Experimental Psychology*. New York: Appleton, Century, Crofts, 1949.

Brooks, Peter. *Reading for the Plot: Design and Intention in Narrative*. New York: Random, 1985.

Chambers, Ross. *Story and Situation: Narrative Seduction and the Power of Fiction.* Theory and History of Literature 12. Minneapolis: University of Minnesota Press, 1984.

Chatman, Seymour. *Story and Discourse: Narrative Structure in Fiction and Film.* Ithaca: Cornell University Press, 1978.

Cohen, Ralph. "History and Genre," *New Literary History* 17.2 (1986) 203-218.

Cohn, Dorrit. "Psyche and Space in Musil's 'Vollendung der Liebe.'" *Germanic Review* 49 (1974) 154-168.

---------- *Transparent Minds: Narrative Modes for Presenting Consciousness in Fiction.* Princeton: Princeton University Press, 1978.

Corino, Karl. *Robert Musils 'Vereinigungen': Studien zu einer historisch-kritischen Ausgabe.* München: Fink, 1974.

Eibl, Karl. "Die dritte Geschichte: Hinweise zur Struktur von Robert Musils Erzählung 'Die Amsel.'" *Poetica* 3 (1970), 455-471.

Ellis, John M. *Narration in the German Novelle.* New York, London: Cambridge University Press, 1974.

Encyclopedia of Philosophy. Ed. Paul Edwards. New York: Macmillan, 1967.

Erickson, Susan. "The Psychopoetics of Narrative in Robert Musil's 'Die Portugiesin.'" *Monatshefte* 78 (1986) 2:167-181.

Fischer, Nanda. "'Eine plötzliche und umgrenzt bleibende geistige Erregung': Zum Novellenbegriff Robert Musils." *Monatshefte* 65 (1973) 3:224-240.

Fowler, Alistair. *Kinds of Literature: An Introduction to the Theory of Genres and Modes*. Cambridge: Harvard University Press, 1982.

Freud, Sigmund. "Das Unheimliche." *Gesammelte Werke* 12. Frankfurt: Fischer, 1952.

Goethe, Johann Wolfgang von. "Nachlese zu Aristoteles' Poetik." *Werke*. Hamburger Ausgabe 12, 9. Aufl. München: Beck, 1981.

Heftrich, Eckhard. *Musil*. München, Zürich: Artemis, 1986.

Henninger, Peter. "Schreiben und Sprechen: Robert Musils Verhältnis zur Erzählform am Beispiel von 'Drei Frauen' und 'Die Amsel.'" *Modern Austrian Literature* 9.3/4 (1976) 57-99.

---------- "'Wissenschaft' und 'Dichtung' bei Musil und Freud." *Modern Language Notes* 94 (1979) 541-568.

Hickmann, Hannah. *Robert Musil and the Culture of Vienna*. London: Croom Helm, 1984.

Hirsch, E. D. *Validity in Interpretation*. New Haven: Yale University Press, 1967.

Hoffmeister, Werner. "Die deutsche Novelle und die amerikanische 'Tale': Ansätze zu einem gattungstypologischen Vergleich." *German Quarterly* 63.1 (1990) 33-49.

Holland, Norman. "Unity Identity Text Self," in *Reader-Response Criticism: From Formalism to Post-Structuralism*. Ed. Jane P. Tompkins. Baltimore: Johns Hopkins University Press, 1980, 118-133.

Iser, Wolfgang. *The Act of Reading*. Baltimore: Johns Hopkins University Press, 1978.

---------- "Indeterminacy and the Reader's Response." In *Aspects of Narrative*. Ed. J. Hillis Miller. New York: Columbia University Press, 1971, 12.

Jakobson, Roman. "On Realism in Art." In: *Readings in Russian Poetics: Formalist and Structuralist Views*. Ed. Ladislav Matejka and Krystyna Pomorska. Cambridge: Harvard University Press, 1971, 38-46.

Jameson, Fredric. *The Political Unconscious: Narrative as a Socially Symbolic Act*. Ithaca: Cornell University Press, 1981.

Jennings, Michael W. "Mystical Selfhood, Self-Delusion, Self-Dissolution: Ethical and Narrative Experimentation in Robert Musil's 'Grigia.'" *Modern Austrian Literature* 17.1 (1984) 59-77.

Kayser, Wolfgang. *Entstehung und Krise des modernen Romans*. Stuttgart: Metzler, 1968.

Köhler, Wolfgang. *Gestalt Psychology*. New York: Liveright, 1929. *

Lanser, Susan Sniader. *The Narrative Act: Point of View in Prose Fiction*. Princeton: Princeton University Press, 1981.

Lucente, Gregory. *The Narrative of Realism and Myth*. Baltimore: Johns Hopkins University Press, 1981.

Luft, David. *Robert Musil and the Crisis of European Culture*. Berkeley: University of California Press, 1980.

Lukács, Georg. *Die Theorie des Romans*. Berlin, 1920. In *Novelle*. Hrsg. Josef Kunz. Wege der Forschung 55. Darmstadt: Wissenschaftliche Buchgesellschaft, 1968, 90-92.

Mae, Michiko. *Motivation und Liebe: Zum Strukturprinzip der Vereinigung bei Robert Musil*. Musil-Studien 16. München: Wilhelm Fink, 1988.

Mandelbaum, Maurice. "Family Resemblances and Generalizations Concerning the Arts." *American Philosophical Quarterly* 2 (1965) 3:219-228.

Martini, Fritz. "Die deutsche Novelle im 'bürgerlichen Realismus': Überlegungen zur geschichtlichen

Bestimmung des Formtypus." *Wirkendes Wort* (1960) 257-278.

McCall, Raymond J. *Phenomenological Psychology: An Introduction.* Madison: University of Wisconsin, 1983.

Monti, Claudia. "Die Mach-Rezeption bei Hermann Bahr und Robert Musil." *Musil-Forum* 10 (1984) 201-213.

Nietzsche, Friedrich. *Werke.* Hrsg. Giorgio Colli und Mazzino Montinari. Vol. 6. Berlin: de Gruyter, 1968.

Novelle, hrsg. Josef Kunz. Wege der Forschung 55. Darmstadt: Wissenschaftliche Buchgesellschaft, 1968.

Nutting, Peter. "Uncaging Musil's 'Amsel.'" *PMLA* 98 (1983) 1: 47-59.

Otto, Rudolph. *The Idea of the Holy.* Tr. John W. Harvey. 2nd ed. London: Oxford University Press, 1957.

Paulin, Roger. *The Brief Compass: The Nineteenth-Century Novelle.* Oxford: Clarendon Press, 1985.

Poe, Edgar Allan. "The Poetic Principle" and "Principles of Composition." In *Poe's Poems and Essays.* Ed. Andrew Lang. 1927, rpr. London: Dent, 1958.

Potts, L. J. *Aristotle on the Art of Fiction: An English Translation of Aristotle's 'Poetics.'* Cambridge: Cambridge University Press, 1968.

Ricoeur, Paul. *The Rule of Metaphor: Multidisciplinary Studies of the Creation of Meaning in Language.* Tr. Robert Czerny. Toronto: University of Toronto Press, 1981.

Rosmarin, Adena. *The Power of Genre.* Minneapolis: University of Minnesota Press, 1985.

Roth, Marie-Louise. "'Die Amsel': Ein Interpretations- versuch." In *Robert Musil--Literatur, Philosophie, Psychologie.* Hrsg. Josef und Johann Strutz. Musil-Studien 12. München: Fink, 1984, 173-186.

---------- *Robert Musil, Ethik und Ästhetik: Zum theoretischen Werk des Dichters.* München: List, 1972.

Röttger, Brigitte. *Erzählexperimente: Studien zu Robert Musils 'Drei Frauen' und 'Vereinigungen.'* Bonn: Bouvier, 1973.

Ryder, Frank G. *Die Novelle.* San Francisco: Rinehart Press, 1971.

Sartre, Jean Paul. *What Is Literature?* Tr. Bernard Frechtman. Gloucester, MA: P. Smith, 1978.

Schaffnit, Hans Wolfgang. *Mimesis als Problem: Studien zu einem ästhetischen Begriff der Dichtung aus Anlaß Robert Musils.* Berlin: de Gruyter, 1971.

Schlegel, August Wilhelm. "Vorlesungen über schöne Literatur und Kunst." Dritter Teil (1803-04). In *Novelle.* Hrsg. Josef Kunz. Wege der Forschung 55. Darmstadt: Wissenschaftliche Buchgesellschaft, 1968, 44-50.

Schlegel, Friedrich. "Nachricht von den poetischen Werken des Johannes Boccaccio." (1801). In *Novelle.* Hrsg. Josef Kunz. Wege der Forschung 55. Darmstadt: Wissenschaftliche Buchgesellschaft, 1968, 39-43.

Schröder, Jürgen. "Am Grenzwert der Sprache: Zu Robert Musils 'Vereinigungen.'" *Euphorion* 60 (1966) 311-334.

Schunicht, Manfred. "Der 'Falke' am 'Wendepunkt': Zu den Novellentheorien Tiecks und Heyses." *Germanisch-Romanische Monatsschrift* 1 (1960) 44-65.

Seidler, Ingo. "Das Nietzschebild Robert Musils." In *Nietzsche und die deutsche Literatur.* Ed. Bruno Hillebrand. Tübingen: Niemeyer, 1978, 160-185.

Shklovsky, Victor. "Art as Technique." In *Russian Formalist Criticism: Four Essays.* Tr. Lee T. Lemon and Marion J. Reis. Lincoln: University of Nebraska Press, 1965, 3-24.

Sokel, Walter H. "Frozen Sea and River of Narration: The Poetics behind Kafka's 'Breakthrough.'" *New Literary History* 17.2 (1986) 351-363.

---------- "Kleists 'Marquise von O.,' Kierkegaards 'Abraham' und Musils 'Tonka': Drei Stufen des Absurden in seiner Beziehung zum Glauben." In *Robert Musil: Studien zu seinem Werk.* Hrsg. K. Dinklage, E. Albertsen, K. Corino. Hamburg: Rowohlt, 1970, 57-70.

---------- "Robert Musils Kampf um die Mimesis: Zur Poetologie seiner Anfänge." *Musil-Forum* 10 (1984) 238-241.

Stanzel, Franz K. *Typische Formen des Romans.* 3. Aufl. Göttingen: Vandenhoeck & Ruprecht, 1967.

Swales, Martin. *The German 'Novelle.'* Princeton: Princeton University Press, 1977.

Todorov, Tzvetan. "The Origin of Genres." *New Literary History* 8.1 (1976) 159-170.

Venturelli, Aldo. "Die Kunst als fröhliche Wissenschaft: Zum Verhältnis Musils zu Nietzsche." *Nietzsche-Studien* 9 (1980) 302-337.

---------- *Robert Musil und das Projekt der Moderne.* Europäische Hochschulschriften. Frankfurt: Lang, 1988.

Weißberg, Liliane. "Versuch einer Sprache des Möglichen: Zum Problem des Erzählens bei Robert Musil." *Deutsche Vierteljahresschrift* 54 (1980) 464-484.

176   K.A. O'Connor

Wicht, Gérard. *'Gott meint die Welt keineswegs wörtlich':* Zum Gleichnisbegriff in Robert Musils Roman 'Der Mann ohne Eigenschaften.' Europäische Hochschulschriften 792. Bern: Lang, 1984.

Wiese, Benno von. *Novelle.* 7th ed. Stuttgart: Metzler, 1978.

Zeller, Rosmarie. "'Die Versuchung der stillen Veronika': Eine Untersuchung ihres Bedeutungsaufbaus." In *Sprachästhetische Sinnvermittlung: Robert Musil Symposion Berlin 1980.* Hrsg. Dieter P. Farda und Ulrich Karthaus. Frankfurt, Bern: Lang, 1980, 135-153.

Zima, Peter. "Robert Musils Sprachkritik: Ambivalenz, Polyphonie und Dekonstruktion," *Musil-Studien 13.* München: Wilhelm Fink, 1985.

INDEX

Paradigm, 16, 24, 29, 63, 69, 76, 80, 98, 141
Perception
  challenge of communicating, 71-72
  compared with thought, 68-70
  of events, 49-50
  language and, 66-69
Phenomenological psychology, 43-46
Poe, E. A., 17, 21
"Die Portugiesin," 81-83, 86-95, 114-115, 151, 155
Psychoanalysis, 39, 50
Psychology, 4, 13, 16, 19, 33, 34, 38-40, 43-51, 64-66, 149
Purpose, 6-8, 11-16, 25, 98, 106, 133

Reader
  narrator's role as, 71, 99, 104
  response of 6, 22, 55, 72, 99, 104-107, 128-130
Realism, literary, 30, 62, 73-76
  alternatives to mimetic forms, 56, 57, 72, 77-79
  apparent, posed, 77-79
  contrasting definitions, 56-57, 64
  criterion of Novelle, 17-19

and perception, 46, 69
and portrayal of women, 86-87
retreat from, 78-88, 139
and Russian Formalism, 55-57
and time, 72-73
Receptivity, 72, 106-108, 114-123, 132-136, 161
Reden, 77, 80,139, 153-163
Responsibility, 123-138, 141
Ricoeur, Paul. See Gleichnis

Schlegel, A. W., 16-18, 21-23, 98, 141
Schlegel, Friedrich, 16-17, 18, 102
Self, concept of, 38, 42, 50-51, 83-85, 104, 108-115
  See also Subject
Shklovsky, Victor, 55-56
Short story
  compared with Novelle, 12-13, 21
Simile. See Gleichnis
Structures, schematic, 81-95
Stumpf, Carl, 27, 40, 43-48, 144
Subject, 38, 102-136
Subjectivity
  and objectivity, 15-20, 29, 57-58, 61, 92
  and receptivity, 102-138
  as basis of Novelle, 16, 20-21, 29, 153

ARIADNE PRESS

TRANSLATION SERIES:

February Shadows
By Elisabeth Reichart
Translated by Donna L. Hoffmeister
Afterword by Christa Wolf

Night Over Vienna
By Lili Körber
Translated by Viktoria Hertling
and Kay M. Stone. Commentary
by Viktoria Hertling

The Cool Million
By Erich Wolfgang Skwara
Translated by Harvey I. Dunkle
Preface by Martin Walser
Afterword by Richard Exner

Buried in the Sands of Time
Poetry by Janko Ferk
English/German/Slovenian
English Translation
by Herbert Kuhner

Puntigam or The Art of Forgetting
By Gerald Szyszkowitz
Translated by Adrian Del Caro
Preface by Simon Wiesenthal
Afterword by Jürgen Koppensteiner

Negatives of My Father
By Peter Henisch
Translated and with an Afterword
by Anne C. Ulmer

On the Other Side
By Gerald Szyszkowitz
Translated by Todd C. Hanlin
Afterword by Jürgen Koppensteiner

*I Want to Speak
The Tragedy and Banality
of Survival in
Terezin and Auschwitz*
By Margareta Glas-Larsson
Edited and with a Commentary
by Gerhard Botz
Translated by Lowell A. Bangerte

The Works of Solitude
By György Sebestyén
Translated and with an
Afterword by
Michael Mitchell

Remembering Gardens
By Kurt Klinger
Translated by Harvey I. Dunkle

Deserter
By Anton Fuchs
Translated and with an Afterwor(
by Todd C. Hanlin

From Here to There
By Peter Rosei
Translated and with an Afterwor
by Kathleen Thorpe

The Angel of the West Window
By Gustav Meyrink
Translated by Michael Mitchel

*Relationships
An Anthology of Contemporary
Austrian Literature*
Selected and with an Introductic
by Adolf Opel

STUDIES IN AUSTRIAN LITERATURE, CULTURE, AND THOUGHT